...ight Clearance
for Creatives

A guide for independent publishers and their support providers

Joyce L. Miller & Dr. C. Daniel Miller

Integrated Writer Services, LLC
Denver, Colorado

FIRST PRINT EDITION January 2013
First eBook Edition March 22, 2013

ISBN-13:
978-0-9886440-4-5 paperback, black & white interior
978-0-9886440-0-7 paperback, full color interior
978-0-9886440-1-4 Kindle ebook
978-0-9886440-2-1 ePub ebook
978-0-9886440-3-8 Adobe PDF ebook on CD-ROM
978-0-9886440-5-2 combo full-color paperback & PDF on CD-ROM

LCCN: 2001012345

Published by:
Integrated Writer Services, LLC
Denver, Colorado 80237-2538
www.WriterServices.biz

Cover design by Nick Zelinger, NZ Graphics
Interior print and PDF design by C. Daniel Miller, Integrated Writer Services, LLC
Ebook design by Gary D. Hall, Greystroke Creative
Proofreading by Susan Hindman, Wordwise Editing
Color interior version printed in the USA by Frederic Printing
B&W interior version printed in the USA by CreateSpace

Disclaimer

While all information in these materials is believed to be correct at the time of writing, the material is intended to alert readers to issues and to educate and inform readers, but is not intended as legal advice. Sometimes, further details may be necessary for a complete understanding of the information in these materials.

If you require legal advice, you should consult an attorney.

INTRODUCTION

The purpose of this guide is to aid authors and publishers and their support teams consisting of writers, editors, photographers, cover designers, interior layout designers, ebook designers, and project managers in their search for and use of good existing legal content created by others. It is also to enable them to protect their own content and control its uses.

New technologies offer new ways to make content readily available to many people. They have also brought changes in ways of viewing content ownership and in methods of ensuring that the works of creative people are protected while, at the same time, making them widely available to those who would enjoy and benefit from them.

The authors have relied on their decades of experience as writers, editors, intellectual property managers, permissions acquisitions consultants, and educators to develop this guide. The guide covers processes and procedures for locating existing content that will add value to current works, for determining if permission is needed for use of the content, and for obtaining permissions when it is advisable to do so. We also discuss some new approaches to copyright protection, define new terms related to copyright, and delineate new procedures for licensing of content—procedures that writers, publishers, and their support teams may find helpful when using the work of others or sharing their own work.

Treatment of URLs

For the most part, the syntax of URLs in this book excludes the "http://" scheme and starts the URL address with "www" except when the URL does not start with "www" after the "http://" scheme. An example of this exception is http://catalog.loc.gov.

CONTENTS

FIGURES

PART 1: INFRINGEMENT–RULES AND RISKS

Scan the QR code below to access a free download of the "Common Misconceptions" listed in Chapter 1.

Chapter 1: The Consequences

Common Misconceptions

Sometimes a work's owner cannot be found or simply will not reply to requests for permission to use their work. Sometimes an owner will deny a request. Users of copyrighted works may decide, when faced with any of these situations, to use the content anyway, telling themselves they will rely on a claim of *fair use* if they face accusations of infringement. This may be the right decision in some cases, but it may have very unpleasant consequences in others. A self-publisher should weigh the risks before using copyrighted material without clearing the rights for their use.

Below are some common misconceptions about copyright law that can get you into trouble. **None of these statements are true!**

Myth: No one sues.
It is a common misconception that no one ever gets sued for using copyrighted materials without permission. Another one is that only people with "deep pockets" get sued. The public isn't aware of many cases that are related to copyright infringement because they are settled out of court. If you are a user or an owner of copyrighted works, you should know that creators of works found to be infringing on copyrighted material may sometimes be required to destroy these works, remove them from bookstore shelves, and be denied any means to share their work with the public. It is true also that settlements may include large payments to the copyright owners and that accused infringers may end up paying hefty attorney fees for negotiations leading to these settlements.

Myth: The chances of my infringements being discovered are minimal.
Another misconception is that a copyright owner likely will never see a copyright infringement. The chances that the content owner will discover any infringement are better than they once were. Today, technology has given creators several ways of discovering infringing uses. Any buzz the infringing work creates will likely find its way to the Internet. Even infringing copied excerpts from a textual work or any instances of infringing derivative artwork in a print work could be scanned and copied into digital format for sharing online, thus tipping off the copyright owner who now has at his fingertips some very effective copyright detection software. The infringer's indiscretion could then become a matter of public record. See Chapter 20 for more information.

CAUTION: The chances of copyright infringements finding their way to the content owner's attention are better than they once were.

Myth: As long as I give attribution, I am not guilty of infringing.
See the definitions of copyright infringement, attribution, and plagiarism in the Glossary. You can be guilty of copyright infringement even though you have given credit. Attribution is not a defense against copyright infringement.

Myth: If it's on the Internet, it's free to use.
See *Cooks Source* Controversy in the Copyright Cases section.

Myth: Royalty-free items are free to use at no cost.
See the definition of royalty free in the Glossary.

Myth: I am not infringing if I paraphrase.
A license to copy is not a license to paraphrase a textual work or alter an illustration. A permission grant to copy a work does not carry with it permission to leave sections out, change words, or add to or subtract from an image unless the license contains a statement allowing such changes. See the definition of *paraphrase* and the discussion on paraphrasing in Chapter 11.

Myth: If I have permission to use an item, I also have permission to paraphrase it.
Paraphrasing is often specifically disallowed in permissions agreements. Permissions agreement terms many times state that no alteration may be made to the original work. Even if no such statement is included in the agreement, if there is no statement specifically allowing it, paraphrasing could precipitate an infringement claim. See Chapter 11 for further discussion.

Myth: It's always okay to use, without permission, a photograph of an old work that is no longer under copyright.
Although there is controversy about when a photograph of a public domain work may be seen as copyrightable, use caution in determining whether to use such a photo. See Bridgeman in the Copyright Cases section.

Myth: Using a portion of another's work when creating a collage always falls in the fair use category.
There is no law that allows a specific amount of an artwork to qualify as fair use. A small but recognizable section of a painting may be considered too much. See "Factor 3, Visual art" in Chapter 5.

Myth: An artist can copy an artwork without permission if it is copied into another medium.
See the discussions of Fairey v. Associated Press and Rogers v. Koons in the Copyright Cases section.

Myth: I can mail myself a copy of my work and use the postmarked date on the package as proof of copyright.

This is called a poor man's copyright. This is not a reliable way of protecting your work. There is no guarantee that it may be offered as evidence in a court of law. Also, remember that you may not bring suit against someone in the United States until you have registered it with the federal government. If you fail to register it within 90 days of its publication, your ability to recover significant damages will be limited.

Myth: As long as I get permission from one entity that has partial ownership of the copyright to an item, I am free and clear to use it.

Many works have multiple owners. You may be required to seek permission from each owner for various aspects of the works or for the works as a whole. Different owners may administer rights for use of content in specific formats. One owner/administrator may issue rights for content use in a print book, but another owner/administrator may issue rights for its use in a digital version.

Myth: If there is no copyright notice on the work, I am free to use it without permission.

No notice is required for copyright protection. The requirement was dropped when the United States joined the Berne Convention, effective March 1, 1989. (This is not to suggest that you should not protect your work by putting a notice on it. Its presence on your work may offer you protection against a defense of innocent infringement if you find it necessary to sue an infringer.)

Myth: Using a line or two of any work doesn't ever require permission.

A line taken from a 300-page novel might be considered infringement if the copying goes to the heart of the work—that is, if it is essential to the theme or message of the work and is seen to be creative enough to warrant protection. See "Factor 3, Text" in Chapter 5.

Myth: Copying someone's work into a textbook or a book with a purpose to inform would most certainly be determined to be a fair use in a court of law.

Some consideration for fair use, when the purpose is to inform, may be given for news articles and book and movie critiques, but it is unlikely that a defense of fair use in copying a substantial amount of content into a textbook would be successful. See the discussion of "The Four Fair Use Factors" in Chapter 5.

Some of the Consequences of Infringement

- If the person accused of infringing is lucky, only a standard fee required of all requestors for a nonexclusive use may be charged. However, there is no guarantee that a fee for an infringing work won't be much higher than the standard fee for the use.
- Someone found to be infringing may have to pay a considerable amount in damages and legal fees. Payment of fees of up to $30,000 per infringing use may be required and, if the court finds the infringement was willful, the fee amounts can climb upward to $150,000 per infringing use. (See the US Constitution, Section 504, Title 17 of the United States Code.)
- The infringement lawsuit could drag out for months, even years, tying the author's hands in regard to the further sale and distribution of the work.
- There could be an order to halt the production and/or distribution of an infringer's work. An infringer who refuses to comply may face a lawsuit. Of course, this order may be less of a problem if the infringing work is distributed only in digital format. Removal of the offending material is much easier and thus the cost is usually more bearable than if the work is in another form such as a fine art poster, a commercial print illustration, or a print book. However, court-ordered alteration of even a digital work after it has been distributed can be damaging to the career and reputation of its creator. And some owners bristle more quickly if something from one of their print works has been digitized by someone else without permission, because they see easy dissemination of digital works as more of a threat than if it had been copied without permission into someone else's print work.

 CAUTION: Selling, or even merely sharing, a work on the Internet that contains content not yet in the public domain in another country could lead to a lawsuit for infringement in that country. A publisher of infringing content could also be sued in the United States for infringing on a work still under copyright in another country.

Chapter 2: Know Who's Responsible

It is important for the self-publisher and members of the support team to know who can be held responsible for infringing. Below is a list of entities that can be held liable for copyright infringement.

1. A company
2. Any individuals working for a company that participates in the infringing act
3. A publisher
4. Anyone who encourages or authorizes infringement

Many of us are self-publishing today, whether in a print or digital medium or in an audio format. This activity likely makes us solely liable for any infringement that may occur in our publications. If you are a self-publisher, you may have no one to filter your work and point out your mistakes regarding copyright infringement. Traditional publishers engage permissions editors who have expertise in catching many indiscretions related to copyright infringement. Some freelance editors are copyright-savvy enough to point out egregious copyright violations, but may miss some infringements that require more comprehensive knowledge of the research and writing known only to the author.

Traditional publishers and some print-on-demand (POD) companies often take another cautious step—that of requiring a statement from their authors that they have cleared copyright, attempting with that requirement to place total responsibility for infringement on the shoulders of their authors.

Remember, creating a blog or website and using the Internet as your means of dissemination to the public makes you a publisher and makes you responsible for copyright infringements on your site. It's important to use caution when you or contributors to your site publish any photograph, text, or artwork on your site. You should determine if the work is copyrighted and if you or your contributors have received permission for its use—or need to request it.

It is wise for self-publishers in the digital and print worlds to learn about copyright and make it a practice to do what they can to keep their work clear of infringing material as well as protect it from abuse by others.

For some court decisions regarding infringement, see the Copyright Cases section.

TIP: Follow the blog at TheCopyrightDetective.com for periodic discussions of recent cases of infringement.

Scan the QR code below to go to The Copyright Detective's blog where you will see discussions of timely topics.

Chapter 3: Know Rights Attached to Ownership

Copyright law protects the following: original works of authorship including literary, dramatic, musical, and artistic works such as poetry, novels, movies, songs, computer software, and architecture.

Copyright law does not protect the following: ideas, short phrases, facts, concepts, systems, and methods of doing something. Use of these elements may break other laws, though. Don't assume that because any use is free of copyright infringement concerns, it is lawful in every other way. A use may be deemed illegal in other areas of law relating to unfair business practices, defamation, publicity laws, privacy laws, and trademark laws.

Copyright owners have the following rights:

1. To reproduce
2. To publish
3. To adapt
4. To distribute

Copyright law was created for the advancement of knowledge. Copyright is the set of exclusive rights granted to the creator of an original work fixed in a tangible form. Copyright law actually gives the creator a *limited monopoly* in order to encourage the creation of new works for the betterment of society. Article I, Section 8 of the US Constitution says the Congress shall have power "to promote the progress of science and the useful arts, by securing for limited times to authors and inventors the exclusive rights to their respective writings and discoveries."

 CAUTION: Some uses of copyrighted content that do not run afoul of copyright law may break other laws having to do with such issues as unfair business practices and defamation, as well as publicity laws, privacy laws, and trademark laws.

Scan the QR code below to get free downloads of amendments to the US Copyright Law since 1976.

Chapter 4: Licenses and Agreements

      In today's world of self-publishing, where authors or freelancers who are members of an author's support team take on responsibility to keep all aspects of a publication legal, it is important they have a basic knowledge of the most common licenses and agreements covering copyrighted material. What follows is a list of suggestions and cautions regarding licenses and agreements.

1. Terms and conditions posted on a site constitute an agreement between users and the site's host. Be sure that you or contributors to your publications are not plagiarizing and/or infringing on work posted elsewhere by someone else. If you are accepting submissions to your blog, in your newsletter, or on your website, you may want to consider including, in a statement of terms and conditions, instructions to contributors regarding submitting to your publication only material that is not infringing on the copyright of others.

Consider a warning such as this

      for a website or blog:
      It is copyright infringement to upload copyrighted content to this site or download copyrighted content from this site without the copyright owner's permission. Do not post content to this site that is copyrighted without first obtaining permission from the owner to do so. Please give proper attribution for all content you post on this site.

      for a newsletter (print or online):
      All third-party copyrighted content being submitted to this publication must have copyright clearance before acceptance. Please sign and attach to your submission the form we have provided, which states that no content you are submitting is infringing on another's copyright.

2. Also read use instructions on sites belonging to others before copying content to publish for any reason. As an example of site instructions on content use, see Appendix C. The web pages (taken from Google) in this appendix model how to examine and give instructions regarding when and how web pages containing copyrighted text and images can be used. Note that these copyrighted Google images and the text are explanations of how to use Google pages and are not to be confused with images belonging to other entities that may be found using the Google

search engine. Any images found through the Google search engine may be copyrighted by their owners and may appear with a copyright notice. However, the exclusion of a notice does not mean these images are without copyright protection. It's best to determine ownership and ask for permission. Such an infringing use may be discovered quickly. There are services now that easily locate infringing material on the Internet.

Sites offering images, such as The Commons on Flickr and the Library of Congress (LOC), are wonderful resources, but understanding the restriction statements on each such site is important. *No known restrictions* is a common statement on these sites. It means that the institution offering this photo for use or viewing has no knowledge of any restrictions. The LOC states that its use of this phrase means the following:

a. There was a copyright and it was not renewed, or

b. The image is from a late nineteenth or early twentieth century collection for which there is no evidence of any rights holder:

- There are no copyright markings or other indications on the images to indicate that they were copyrighted or otherwise restricted, AND
- The records of the US Copyright Office do not indicate any copyright registration, AND
- The acquisition paperwork for the collection does not contain any evidence of any restrictions, AND
- Images from the collection have been used and published extensively without anyone stepping forward to claim rights.

The LOC further states, "These facts do not mean the image is in the public domain, but do indicate that no evidence has been found to show that restrictions apply."

The institutions will not warrant that some uses of such images is legal, and the onus is on the user to determine the risks of using content labeled with this phrase. However, the LOC states, "The Library is unaware of any lawsuits involving the use of its historical images." (This explanation and much more valuable information about using images is at www.loc.gov/rr/print/195_copr.html#catalog.)

3. A license to copy is not a license to paraphrase a textual work or alter an illustration. A permission grant to copy a work does not carry with it permission to leave sections out, change words, or add to or subtract from an image, unless the license contains a statement allowing such changes.

4. Multiple copyrights may exist in some content. Get all necessary releases. This may mean making requests to several owners for permission. Song lyrics, for example, may have several writers and rights administrators. Photos may contain copyrighted artwork or people's images

(requiring model releases). Figures, illustrations, and contributions to periodicals may require permission from their creators, and the article author or periodical publisher may or may not be able to help you locate these owners, especially if the publication from which you are taking the content is more than a year old.

5. Possession or purchase of a physical work such as a photograph or painting does not imply ownership of the copyright on it and the right to publish it.

6. Clearance of the rights for one format, territory, or language does not allow for use in any other formats, territories, or languages.

7. Click agreements are licenses. They require the website user to click assent to the terms of use of a site by clicking on a button containing the words *Okay; OK; Yes, I Agree;* or similar language. Since these agreements contain limitations on use, they should be read carefully, and each stipulation should be followed.

8. Giving credit for copyrighted content does not excuse using another's work without permission. Attribution is not a defense for infringement. A person giving proper attribution will not be guilty of *plagiarism,* but copying another's work without permission, even though attribution is made, can be an act of *copyright infringement.*

9. Royalty-free agreements often have a cost attached to them. With these agreements, a publisher may pay for the use of items in a printed collection of images, online access to a number of images, or for a digital collection containing a number of images. The publisher may then use each item available for download or in the digital collection on a delivery media such as CDs and DVDs. This use must be in a manner the license specifies.

10. Several different types of Creative Commons licenses are generally used. It's wise to study the limitations of each Creative Commons license before using any content it covers (see Appendix F).

11. Images found through Google searches should not be used like a stock photo service. There are warnings on the Google search results that these images may be copyrighted. **Copyrighted images are infringed upon more than any other kind of content on the web.** Google's Advanced Image Search provides an option titled "usage rights" to search images that are free to use and share.

12. The fact that a technology allows an online activity is no reason to assume its use constitutes a fair use. Some such online activities are infringement; others aren't. See below.

Hypertext linking
A URL is like a street address and cannot be copyright protected. However, a list or collection of URLs may be protected. Individual URLs can, in most instances, be linked to without a risk

of claims of infringement, but the copiers should be sure they have permission before they copy and distribute a collection of URLs. Creating a hyperlink is usually not in itself an infringing act.

 CAUTION: Linking to an infringing website may be perceived as authorizing and encouraging infringement. See an example of consequences of such linking in the Copyright Cases section about extradition procedures against Richard O'Dwyer.

Deep linking

Deep linking may be considered by some courts to be infringement. A deep link is a link that bypasses the home page of another website. For example, the *Washington Post* offers instruction on linking to them in their copyright notice. *Time* magazine's website includes instruction on digital sharing on their Terms and Conditions of Use page.

Framing

Framing describes the practice of importing content onto a web page from another website and displaying it in a frame that makes it appear to originate on the site importing it. This technique can imply endorsement, and it alters the appearance of the original page. Framing has been found in some court cases to be infringement.

Inline linking

Inlining is incorporating a graphic file from one website into another website. The graphic is linked to another website but appears on the infringing website. Inlining has been found to be infringement.

Embedding videos found on YouTube may be considered a variation of inline linking since the image of the video frame and the video itself actually resides on YouTube's server. When someone posts a video on YouTube, they must choose to allow or disallow others to embed it on their own website. If you can get the HTML code from YouTube to embed a video, then the person posting the video has enabled embedding the video on other websites. However, embedding someone else's YouTube video into your site can be infringement if the person who posted the video on YouTube did not have permission to do so. Before you do so, be sure the person posting the video has the rights to it.

Web scraping

Web scraping is becoming more prevalent. It is a process that uses computer software techniques for extracting content from a website. It can be used for purposes such as republishing, downloading archives, or extracting images, all of which may be infringement if done without permission from the website owner.

Pinning

Pinterest is a very popular content-sharing service where members can create and manage theme-based collections of images. As long as the images are your own, or you have determined you are copyright compliant in pinning them using the site, you may find the website a good marketing opportunity. Images that are pinned on Pinterest are stored on the website. Pinning an image on this site does not result in a thumbnail image like you see on many sites, but rather a full-size copy in many cases. Pinning copyrighted images here without permission of the owner violates their copyright and can hurt their business. Remember, an image posted on the Internet enjoys the same copyright protection that images in print works enjoy.

Before you pin someone else's image, it would be wise to get a fuller explanation of the damage that pinning copyrighted images can do to photographers, artists, and bloggers and the risks of infringement it can mean for you.

Scan the QR code below to go start exploring the 14,000,000+ images available at the Library of Congress.

PART 2: WHEN YOU DON'T NEED TO ASK–USING OTHERS' WORKS WITHOUT PERMISSION

Scan the QR code below to review the US Copyright Office Factsheet FL102 on "fair use."

Chapter 5: Fair Use

There are two situations in which a writer may legally use others' content without permission. One of these situations occurs when the use is considered a fair use.

Criticism, comment, news reporting, teaching, scholarship, and research fall under fair use (US Copyright Office Factsheet FL102). An understanding of activities involving two of these categories may be useful to self-published authors with websites, blogs, or books that discuss the work of others.

A book reviewer may use a portion of a work in a piece that offers criticism or comment. An art critic may reproduce a photo of an artwork in order to discuss and offer criticism of it. These uses in many cases would be judged as fair uses. (It may minimize the risk of infringement claims for the reviewer, however, to use a thumbnail rather than a full-size photo.)

A parody that uses copied content taken from the work parodied may also be determined to be a fair use. It may be much more difficult for you to determine if a court will rule a work a true parody than to judge whether or not you really have written a critique or a commentary on a copyrighted work. A parody can be a musical, a literary work, or an artwork of fancy that ridicules another work or has an element of social commentary that treats—at least in part—the subject matter of the parodied work. To be considered a parodied work, the work copied usually has to be recognizable by the public—has to be a work that is well known. Many times, it is a court of law that decides if the new work is a parody and thus the inclusion of others' copyrighted material in it a fair use. We would caution self-publishers to seek an attorney's advice before publishing what they determine to be a parody unless they are very savvy about copyright issues.

When trying to determine if a use is a fair use, it's helpful to remember the goal of copyright law: to encourage the creation of new works for the betterment of society. If a work based on another work is transformative enough—that is, if the new use of the original work transforms it into something new, unique, and that is a benefit to society in some way—it is more likely to be considered by a court of law to be a fair use.

For a court case involving a photograph and a sculpture that highlights issues with claims of parody, see Rogers v. Koons. For a case with claims of parody involving a literary work, see Salinger v. Colting. Both are in the Copyright Cases section.

TIP: The US Copyright Office has a number of resources available to assist in the process of registering copyrights and using copyrighted materials. One of these resources is Factsheet FL102, *which contains an explanation of US copyright law. The URL for the complete factsheet on fair use is: www.copyright.gov/fls/fl102.html.*

CAUTION: Fair use is a legal doctrine that allows the use of copyrighted works without permission under certain conditions and with certain limitations. It is often difficult to predict a finding of fair use, as you can see from the discussion below, so we usually advise our clients to weigh the risk of using without permission any content they are not fairly certain fits into a fair use category. We suggest they attempt to secure permission when uncertain; in cases where they cannot locate the owner of content, or permission is denied, we suggest they do a risk analysis using the information below before they decide to include the item in their work.

The Four Fair Use Factors

Section 107 of Title 17 of the United States Code includes four fair use factors that were created to offer guidance in deciding fair use:

1. The purpose and character of the use

2. The nature of the copied work

3. The amount and substantiality of the portion used

4. The effect on potential market for the original work

Factor 1: Purpose and Character of the Use

A transformative use

Does it offer new information, new meaning, new aesthetics, or new insights and understandings? Does it advance knowledge or spur progress of the useful arts? If so, it is possible that it may be determined a fair use in a court of law.

It helps to understand the reasoning behind this analysis. As previously stated, copyright law was created to advance knowledge. Giving a creator a limited monopoly motivates creativity. However, sometimes there is a use without permission of a copyright-protected work that gives society something new and different (that advances knowledge). In such a case, an exception may be made. The resulting derivative may be given protection, and a fair use defense may be successful in a court of law.

In any transformative use case, a battle is fought between the public benefits to society of allowing the creation and circulation of a derivative work by someone other than its copyright owner and the need to provide incentive and reward in the form of protection (limited monopoly) to the creator of original works so they will create more.

Courts usually view a noncommercial use more positively than a commercial use, partly because of its accessibility to all members of society regardless of their ability to pay for the content.

Factor 2: Nature of Copied Work

Fictional or factual

The more creative the content is seen to be, the more value is placed on it by society and thus by the courts. Therefore, fictional content is usually awarded broader copyright protection than factual content.

Published or unpublished

Being able to decide when and whether to ever publish is one of those exclusive rights of copyright law, and this right to decide is afforded significant protection by the courts. Thus, unpublished works are usually offered broader protection than published works.

Factor 3: Amount

There is **no set amount** of words or **percentage of content** allowed by law as a fair use. It's a common misconception that copying 250 words or less or using up to 15 percent of an artwork to make a derivative is defined in copyright law as a fair use.

Text

If a short paragraph is taken from a 300-page novel, the use might be considered a fair use. However, a line taken from a 300-page novel might be considered infringement if the copying goes to the heart of the work—that is, if it is essential to the theme or message of the work and is seen to be creative enough to warrant protection.

Lyrics/poetry

Even one line of lyrics or a line of poetry may be too much to be considered fair use.

Case in point: The person who wrote a foreword for a client of ours had included in it a few lines of lyrics from a Beatles song. After our client had printed five thousand copies of her book, she was told that there might be some claim of infringement brought against her because of this use without permission. She hoped that it might be considered a fair use. She consulted with attorneys. The attorneys told her using the lyrics in this way without permission could be risky. Integrated Writer Services was able, after the fact, to get permission for a reasonable fee. But things could have gone badly. The client could have been required to remove these books from circulation and pay damages. At any rate, this client suffered several days of anxiety wondering what the outcome would be.

If a rights administrator realizes that a printed work has already been completed, they might charge a much higher fee for the use of the original content because they see the infringer's dilemma and realize that they may be willing to pay a high fee rather than pull their works from circulation. Attorneys' fees in such a scenario can be quite high as well. It's best to avoid such uncertainty. Get permission.

John Lennon's handwritten lyrics to the Beatles song "A Day in the Life" recently sold for $1.2 million. When works have such high value attached to them, the risks involved in using them are most often much higher than one might imagine.

Visual art

There is no law that allows a specific amount of an artwork to qualify as fair use. A small but recognizable section of a painting may be considered too much. There is no art media that is excused as fair use. The creator of a collage using copyrighted work, for example, may not win an infringement case using a fair use defense based on the fact that the work is a collage. Copying even a small amount of someone else's work into a collage could be considered an infringement.

Factor 4: Effect on Potential Market

If the use currently deprives the owner of income, or if the possibility exists that it may deprive the owner of future income, it will likely not be considered in a court of law as a fair use. Possible future uses are often included in the consideration of this factor. These future uses include new projects based on the original work such as series, supplements, and guides to the work.

The Difficulty in Predicting a Finding of Fair Use

There may be a certain level of risk involved in using the works of others without permission based on a guess that a court finding of fair use will excuse this use. Some reasons for avoiding leaning too heavily on a fair use argument follow:

1. In copyright litigation, each case is fact specific. The four fair use factors in the US Code

couldn't possibly address the particulars of all cases. US Copyright Office Factsheet FL-102 elaborates on fair use.

2. All four fair use factors are not given equal weight in each case. No one can safely say that any use will be considered fair by a court of law. There is no way of determining beforehand how these four factors will be weighed or the outcome of a court case.

3. There is another fact that highlights the difficulties in predicting the outcome of a case involving a claim of fair use. That is, when a case is appealed and moves to a higher court, the lower court's decision is often reversed. The Supreme Court, when hearing an appeal from such a case, could reverse the decision once again and decide as the lower court initially had done.

Public domain images abound. Scan the QR code below to go to Wikipedia's listing of public domain resources.

Chapter 6: Public Domain

The second situation where content created by others may be used without permission is when the original work is in the public domain. Below is some general information that may help you determine if a work is in the public domain. In some cases, you may quickly find that the work you wish to use is definitely in the public domain. In other cases, more research will be required to determine the work's status.

CAUTION: Sometimes, determining if a work is in the public domain can be done quickly and with relative ease. BUT discovering with certainty that a work is in the public domain sometimes requires more information than is given here. In-depth discussions outlining all the issues involved in finding the answer to certain questions about an expiration date for a specific work is beyond the scope of this guide.

Definition of Public Domain

The US Copyright Office provides the following definition of *public domain*, for guidance on this confusing and often incorrectly applied concept:

> *The public domain is not a place. A work of authorship is in the "public domain" if it is no longer under copyright protection or if it failed to meet the requirements for copyright protection. Works in the public domain may be used freely without the permission of the former copyright owner.*
> *(Source: www.copyright.gov/help/faq/faq-definitions.html)*

Content is in the public domain if any one of the following descriptions is true.

1. Its copyright has expired.
2. It was created by federal government employees as part of their duties.
3. It does not qualify for copyright.
4. It was placed into the public domain by the owner (through a Creative Commons license, for example).

 CAUTION: Some government sites may contain privately owned materials the government licensed. The site should clearly note that such materials were not created by a government employee and are not within the public domain.

Determining if the Work Is in the Public Domain

This chapter will be helpful to those who think the work they wish to use may be in the public domain. The first place to look for copyright renewal information is on the copyright page of any work that contains one. See the copyright page of this guidebook as an example.

If no information is given within the publication about a renewal, the places to begin a search to find out if a work is in the public domain may be the sources listed below. Such a search is a good way to identify some works as needing permission. The tools given at the end of this chapter also offer quick help in determining if a work is in the public domain.

 CAUTION: If the work's copyright registration requires renewal to retain the copyright and it has been renewed, permission may be needed to use that work. If the sources below contain no record that a registration requiring a renewal has been renewed, in some circumstances it may still be copyrighted. If it appears a work requiring renewal has not been renewed and it is something you wish to use, you may decide to seek guidance about its status from an attorney or from a permissions consultant.

Publication Dates and Renewals

The easiest public domain reference date to remember is that books published in the United States before 1923 are in the public domain. Information about dates of publication and renewals of copyrighted text and still images can be found at the Library of Congress by going to the US Copyright Office website (www.copyright.gov) and clicking on *Search the Catalog*, by consulting the duration chart at the Cornell University website (http://copyright.cornell.edu/resources/publicdomain.cfm), by using an Amazon search for specific titles, or by searching the Stanford University Copyright Renewal Database (http://copyright.cornell.edu/resources/publicdomain.cfm), the University of Pennsylvania's Online Books Page Copyright Registration and Renewal Records website (www.digital.library.upenn.edu/books/cce/), and Google's scans of the Catalog of Copyright Entries (http://books.google.com/googlebooks/copyrightsearch.html).

Some of these sites, which are discussed in the following subsections, contain renewals of books published between 1923 and 1963, the period of greatest confusion for when books go into the public domain. Books published in the United States between these dates must have been renewed twenty-eight years after their initial publication in order to retain copyright protection. Table 1 illustrates when works go into the public domain.

Published before 1923		Public Domain (PD)
Published 1923–1963 with Notice		
	If not renewed	PD in 28 years from first publication
	If renewed	PD in 95 years from first publication
Published 1964–1977 with Notice		
	Automatic renewal	PD in 95 years from first publication
Created before 1978, published 1978–2002		PD on Jan. 1, 2048
Created after 1978		
	Individual(s) authorship	PD in life of author + 70 years
	Corporate authorship	PD, the shorter of 95 years from publication or 120 years from creation

Table 1: US Copyright Duration of Published Works

Some of the websites mentioned above also contain information for registrations occurring before 1978—information that you will not find online at the US Copyright Office website. If a book was published between 1964 and 1977, it was automatically renewed by statute. If a book was published and registered or renewed in 1978 or later, you should be able to find its registration status in the records online at www.copyright.gov/records.

TIP: Works published in the United States between 1923 and 1964 are the works that need special attention regarding renewals. Works published before 1923 in the United States are in the public domain. Works published after 1964 were automatically renewed and are likely still in copyright.

CAUTION: Because of a quirk in copyright law, if a previously unpublished work was published between 1977 and 2003, its copyright protection now lasts through 2047. For example, some previously unpublished works of Samuel Clemens that were published after 1976 and before 2003 are now copyright protected through 2047.

Using Online Search Sites

Listings of copyright information for books, periodicals, music, and still images such as artwork, maps, commercial prints, and labels are available at a number of locations. Some of them are listed below. Be aware that more and more information on renewals and registration will become available in time and that this list may not be exhaustive.

Stanford University

The Copyright Renewal Database at Stanford University permits searches of copyright renewal records for books published between 1923 and 1963. All of these renewals are not available online at the US Copyright Office website. The Stanford website does not include nonbook renewals or original registrations. Add twenty-eight years to the date of the original publication and search titles in that year to see if the copyright was renewed. For example, Harper Lee's *To Kill a Mockingbird* was originally registered on April 25, 1960, and was renewed on June 13, 1988. It's a good idea to also check the year before and the year after that date. (Source: http://collections.stanford.edu/copyrightrenewals/bin/search/simple/process?query=to+k ill+a+mockingbird)

University of Pennsylvania

The Online Books Page Copyright Registration and Renewal Records at the University of Pennsylvania allows you to search for copyright renewal of books first published between 1923 and 1963. In addition, it allows you to search for renewal of serials and periodicals. Plus, all active renewals for still images (artwork, maps, and commercial prints and labels) are now accessible at this site. (Source: www.digital.library.upenn.edu/books/cce/)

Library of Congress

The Library of Congress provides an online Copyright Catalog that contains copyright records from 1978. Instructions on its use can be found there. Renewals for works registered from 1951 to 1963 can also be found there. Entries for all types of works registered and renewed before 1978 can be found in bound volumes of the Catalog of Copyright Entries (located in major city libraries throughout the country). Go to Appendix A and Appendix B for step-by-step instructions on using the Library of Congress website to search for copyright information.

Google Books

Google Books offers a search of scans of the Catalog of Copyright Entries. This is a full-text search and links to individual volumes of copyright registrations from 1922 to 1977. Here you can find original and renewal registrations for books, pamphlets, and contributions to periodicals during that time period (except for 1952, when only book registrations and renewals are available).

 CAUTION: Later translations of public domain works may still be in copyright.

CAUTION: Plagiarism can hurt your career and/or reputation. Even though the work is in the public domain, it is usually wise and most often ethical to credit its source.

Copyright Term Tables

The copyright term table at the Cornell website is helpful in determining if a work is in the public domain. It even covers works never published and never registered.
(Source: http://copyright.cornell.edu/resources/publicdomain.cfm)

Another chart that you may find helpful is on the University of North Carolina website and is titled *When U.S. Works Pass into the Public Domain*. Its creator is Lolly Gasaway.
(Source: www.unc.edu/~unclng/public-d.htm)

 CAUTION: Works first published outside the United States and that had been for a time in the public domain in this country may have had their copyright restored in the United States with the Copyright Law of 1996. Before you use such foreign works without express permission, you may wish to consult with an attorney.

 CAUTION: A public domain item may be more difficult to use than you imagine because of inaccessibility to the physical item or to photos or copies of it. If the original is in a private collection or a museum, it may be difficult or costly to obtain copies of it with a resolution adequate for printing or computer screen display. And remember, a photo of a public domain item may itself be protected under copyright.

Purchasers of this book may access the Excel permissions tracking logs shown in Part 3. Scan the QR code below to access the web page to access the logs.

PART 3: STEPS IN THE PERMISSION PROCESS

Ever want to create a book trailer free of copyright concerns? Scan the QR code below to access a blog about the process.

Chapter 7: Considerations before Clearing Rights

Below is a list of considerations for creatives who are planning to clear rights to use copyrighted content. Some of them will affect the fees charged for permissions. This book addresses many of these considerations. A consultation with a permissions acquisition expert might be helpful in addressing some of these considerations.

1. How difficult is it going to be to find owners of the copyrighted content I wish to use?
2. Is the value added to my work by each item of copyrighted content I wish to use worth the effort required to obtain permission to use it and the expense I may incur acquiring it?
3. If I do the work, what kind of budget is required to track down administrators and acquire the images or text I am considering using? If I hire someone, what kind of budget is required to track down administrators for the copyrighted content I am considering using?
4. If I decide to acquire rights myself and save on permission acquisition costs, what are the steps in this process?
5. Are there free or low-cost copyrighted content items and public domain content items available that would fit my needs?
6. What rights will I ask for: exclusive or nonexclusive? See the definition in the Glossary.
7. In which territories will my work be distributed? In other words, where will the product I am creating be sold or given away: United States only, North America, specific countries, or worldwide?
8. What price will be charged for the product containing my work? Is there going to be a difference between the price of any electronic and print versions? If so, what will be the price for each version?
9. If my work will be printed, how many copies will I have printed in the first run?
10. How many people will be allowed to access or download my work for any electronic formats? It is important to note that print rights and electronic rights are conferred as separate rights, often with their own fees attached and occasionally administered by separate rights holders.
11. In which languages will the work be distributed in print and/or electronically?
12. If my work is distributed as a print work, will I ask for permission to use copyrighted material for the number of copies in my first run or will I ask for permission to include content in additional copies to cover future runs? Some rights administrators may have a set minimum fee, and it will be for up to a specified number of copies (i.e., five thousand). This number of copies may be far more than you had planned to print. If that is the case, you will have to decide whether to pay the set minimum fee or remove the copyrighted content. If the fee is reasonable, you could ask for permission to print up to the number limit specified for the minimum fee.

13. Am I going to independently publish, print, and distribute my work? Am I going to use a print-on-demand provider? If I am going to be an independent publisher, what is the name of my publishing company?
14. Have I determined an estimated date of publication for my work?
15. If my work is to be offered in an electronic format, have I decided the length of time I will have my work accessible to readers in this format?
16. Has a format, or have multiple formats, been chosen for my work (ebook, online download, POD, print, audiobook, website, blog, etc.)?
17. Is it possible that my work will be distributed in new formats as technology advances, and do I need to get permission now from copyright owners for use of their work in future technologies?
18. In which markets will my work be distributed and/or sold?
19. Is the publication and distribution of my work to be a for-profit or nonprofit venture?
20. If my work or part of my work is a commissioned work, who will own the copyright and who will be held liable if someone sues for copyright infringement? How can I protect myself from a contributor's infringements?
21. How much of my budget will I allow for rights fees?
22. Will the copyrighted content be needed for promotional materials related to the work?
23. Will the copyrighted content be used in any derivative versions of my work?
24. What format(s) will I use to credit the work of others, and where in my work will I place credits? The location and style of credits may be subject to agreement stipulations, in some cases.
25. In which requests will I ask for a warranty that the licensor has the legal right to grant copyright permission and that the content in question does not infringe on the rights of any third parties?
26. Will I purchase rights now for uses that might be made of copyrighted works in the future? Think about your present budget limitations and weigh them against the ease of carrying out future plans without having to go back for additional permissions.
27. Do I have the pertinent publishing information from the edition of the copied work for which I am requesting permission? Administrators want page numbers and sometimes copies of pages you are using. Different editions have different publishers and page-numbering schemes. Administrators will not grant permission for an edition they don't represent.

Chapter 8: Permissions Agreements for Text and Visual Art

This chapter includes descriptions of common components of two types of permissions agreements. The first is for use of text content and the second for use of visual art content. Some publishers provide directions for how requests are to be submitted and what information is to be provided. For example, Random House provides on its website individual forms for eight different uses of its copyrighted content. These forms contain examples of the typical information that is requested in a permissions request.
(Source: www.randomhouse.com/about/permissions.html)

There may be special needs and situations that require additional content not listed in the two agreement descriptions below. These examples are meant as basic guides for the permissions seeker and the permissions grantor.

Text Permissions Agreement

Section 1: Licensor and Licensee

The first section of a text permissions agreement typically identifies the Licensor (owner/administrator of rights to the copyrighted work) and the Licensee (the party asking for permission to use the work).

Section 2: Licensor's Work

The second section may contain details of the work from which you wish to borrow:

- Title of text (or actual selection of text)
- Author(s)
- Source publication (book title, magazine title, website URL, etc.)
- Identifiers for title (ISBN if a book; the ISSN, volume number, issue number, and date if a periodical)
- Page numbers and/or number of pages you wish to use
- Word count of text being requested

Section 3: Licensee's Work

The third section typically contains details about your work:

- Title of your book, article, etc.
- Title of periodical or collection in which your work will appear
- Your website URL if you are placing copied content on your website
- Name of publisher
- Full name of author(s)
- Price of your work
- Estimated date you plan to publish (print, ebook, audiobook) or post (publish via website)
- Estimated number of copies you plan to print or distribute; or the estimated number of visitors per month if you are placing content on a website; or the number of people who will have access to it in a given period of time if you are publishing on an online delivery system

A permissions agreement for a print version and/or digital versions may cover a specified period of time during which you may reproduce print works and distribute digital versions.

Section 4: Grant of Rights

The Grant of Rights section will indicate whether you are being granted exclusive or nonexclusive rights, and may describe the manner in which you may reproduce and distribute your work. Remember, the more rights you request, the higher the usage fee that may be asked. Typical rights include the following:

- The current edition and all subsequent editions of the work
- Any derivatives of the work
- Any language the work is reproduced in: English, Spanish, French, etc.
- All media now known or later devised
- Use in materials promoting your work

The Grant of Rights section may also cover "the territory" and will specify where you may distribute your work if you use the granted materials. It will cover only the territory you have specified in your request or only territories the administrator is willing to give. Choices might be US rights only, world rights, and North American rights. The broader the scope of the territory granted, the higher the permission fee that may be asked.

Section 5: Fees and Duration of Grant

The Fee section will specify an amount based on all the criteria mentioned above. It will probably cover inclusion in a limited number of print and/or ebook copies or delivery to a limited number of viewers if pertaining to an online delivery system version. This section may also contain wording similar to the most favored nations clause. See the definition in the Glossary.

This section may specify the length of time you will be allowed to use a work. It may specify that the use is for one edition or all editions. If use of the reproduced material is for a website, it may allow for use of a period of weeks or months, for example.

Section 6: Attribution

The Attribution section may specify how the administrator prefers the credit to read.

Section 7: Samples

The Samples section will require you to send a specific number of copies of the work to the licensor upon its publication. Typically, one or two copies are requested.

Section 8: Warranty

In this section, the Licensor warrants that it has the right to grant the rights detailed in the agreement.

Section 9: Miscellaneous

The Miscellaneous section may specify what happens if the agreement is found invalid or unenforceable. It may designate which state's laws govern its interpretation.

Visual Art Permissions Agreement

Following are some of the items common to a permissions agreement for an editorial use of visual art (that is, a use on a noncommercial website or as an editorial use in a book). If the use is commercial—in other words, if the use is to sell a product or service—your agreement will probably need to cover more legal issues than are covered here. You may wish to hire an attorney to draft an agreement for art for commercial use.

Section 1: Licensor and Licensee

The first paragraph of a visual art permissions agreement typically identifies the Licensor (owner/administrator of rights to the copyrighted work) and the Licensee (the party asking for permission to use the work).

 CAUTION: If you are contemplating a "work made for hire" agreement, understand that the agreement described in this section is NOT such an agreement. The US Copyright Office's Circular 09 explains the term "work made for hire" under the 1976 Copyright Act. (Source: www.copyright.gov/circs/circ09.pdf)

Section 2: Licensor's Work

The second section may contain details about the work from which you wish to obtain visual art:

- Title of work (painting, illustration, map, photograph, etc.)
- Catalog number, if there is one
- Copyright owner's name

Section 3: Licensee's Work

This section may contain details for your work:

- Title of your book, article, DVD, CD, etc.
- Title of periodical or collection in which your work will appear
- Your website URL if you are placing copied content on your website (Indicate whether the page is a home page or an internal page and if the site is commercial or noncommercial. You may be asked for the average number of visitors to the site per month and the length of time the content will be posted.)
- Name of publisher
- Full name of author(s)
- Price of your work
- Estimated date you plan to publish (print, ebook, audiobook) or first posting if the use is an online use
- Estimated number of copies in a printed book format and an estimate for ebook sales

If you are publishing on an online delivery system, this section may indicate the number of people who will have access to it in a given period of time.

A permissions agreement for a print version and/or digital versions may cover a specified period of time during which you may reproduce print works and distribute digital versions.

Section 4: Grant of Rights

Your choices of rights obtained to reproduce and distribute visual art go in this section. (Remember, choices affect the rates the licensor will be charge for the use.)

Typical rights include the following:

- The current editions of the work
- All foreign language versions of the work
- All derivative versions of the work
- In promotional materials
- Placement, size of image, media, and territory

References to "territory" will specify where you may distribute your work if you use the granted materials. It will cover only the territory you have specified in your request or only territories the administrator is willing to give. Choices might be US rights only, world rights, and North American rights.

Two other choices typically covered in this section regarding rights are exclusive or nonexclusive use of the visual art. The license will indicate which type is given.

Section 5: Fees

The requestor may pay either (1) a flat fee or (2) royalties and an advance. A flat fee is a payment that is made upon execution of the agreement or upon publication of the requestor's work. Be sure that a choice between these two situations is included.

This section may also contain a date by which payment is to be received.

Section 6: Attribution

This section includes the credit the use is to carry and the stipulation that any and all versions of the work that shall include the selection shall contain the credit statement.

Section 7: Samples

This includes a statement that at least one copy of the work containing the new use is to be given to the licensor.

Section 8: Warranty

A warranty includes a statement that the licensor has the right to grant permission for the use as outlined in the agreement.

Section 9: Miscellaneous

The Miscellaneous section may specify what happens if the agreement is found invalid or unenforceable. It may designate the state laws that govern its interpretation.

 CAUTION: Sometimes a permissions agreement will be granted with the stipulation that the author or creator/ all authors or creators of the licensed work grant permission as well. This can occur, for example, when an item has multiple owners or when a periodical publisher is unsure if past contributors to the publication have retained ownership in the work. It is important to read permissions agreements carefully and follow them to the letter!

Chapter 9: Creating a "Permissions Tracking Log"

A "permissions tracking log" simply is a method of systematically recording key information during the process of obtaining permission to use copyrighted materials. If you are only seeking permission for one or two items, a notepad may be sufficient. However, if you are seeking permission to use content from several sources, a spreadsheet will prove a useful way to keep a record of all the variables.

It is wise, also, to start the permissions process as early as possible because it can take weeks and even months to get a response. Before committing to some uses that could make or break your project down the road, attempt to determine if acquiring the permissions you need is going to be possible and if the fees will fit the project budget.

 CAUTION: One fact that brings home the importance of avoiding last-minute roadblocks to your publication caused by copyright issues is that the US Copyright Office charges $445 an hour, with a minimum of 2 hours, to do an expedited search on a work. If you wait until you are ready to publish to determine whether the use of some important content is really legal, you might be facing what could have been an avoidable expense and maybe a finding that puts a hold on publication. For more information, see Circular 4: Copyright Office Fees. The website also contains a number of other useful documents related to copyright issues. (Source: www.copyright.gov/circs/)

You will want to record the following kinds of information regardless of how many items you are seeking.

When you have chosen a copyrighted item to use, you should photocopy the title page, copyright page, acknowledgments page(s) relative to your use, and the page(s) containing the content you plan to use, especially if the source is not something you will have on hand (i.e., library or reference book). You can also enter important details from these pages in your log to more easily keep track of the information.

If you are working with an online source, bookmark the site and file the bookmark under your project name. You also may want to print a copy of the web page with the specific URL noted on the printed copy for your files.

Start filling in the log with information about the source that you gathered off the copyright page and acknowledgments page, website, CD or DVD cover, etc. If you are working from a collection or a book that has borrowed from other sources, keep in mind that it is essential to find the original source of the copyrighted content as early as possible. The secondary source will NOT be able to grant permission. Collections often prove useful by pointing to the original source, but you may save time and money by using the original source to begin with.

It may prove useful to record the dates and content for each person contacted, from the first inquiry to the mailing with the check for the fee and the signed agreement, since you will not know in advance if several contacts will be required. If you are working with several content items, it will be helpful to give a reference number to each one so that you can easily track them.

Appendix H contains graphic examples of specific permissions tracking logs for various kinds of content that you may wish to obtain permission to use.

- Text for print
- Text for ebooks
- Song lyrics
- Photographs
- Periodicals
- Maps, graphs, and figures
- Graphics and fine art
- Comic strips

Excel spreadsheets that may be downloaded and used by purchasers of this guide to track copyright clearance projects may be found at www.TheCopyrightDetective.com/guide/logs.

Chapter 10: Why Have Alternative Choices?

It is wise to identify alternative content in case (1) permission fees are too expensive, (2) it takes too long to get a response to your request, (3) you get no reply from the copyright owner, or (4) permission is denied for your first choice.

Budgetary Concerns

Fees can range from less than $25 to hundreds of dollars per instance. Sometimes permission is granted gratis. As mentioned previously, any agreement that includes a clause with language similar to "most favored nations" can be problematic because the effect is to raise the fees for all similar items to the highest fee charged by any one source. You always have the option to not use the content with the higher fees, of course.

Time Constraints

Many responses will arrive four to six weeks from the time you sent the request, but often a response will take three months and sometimes much longer. Random House now indicates on its website that a requestor should allow a minimum of eight weeks for a response to a request. And it is not that unusual for a response to come back weeks after the initial inquiry indicating that the person you contacted is not the person who can grant rights to use the content.

Nonresponsive Owners and Orphan Works

Some owners of copyrighted content are not responsive. Your permissions log should contain every attempt to contact the owner, including dates and how the attempts to contact were carried out. Your notes in your log regarding these attempts may help to show due diligence on your part.

Some works have owners that cannot be located. These works are called orphan works. Although at times, a claim that an author cannot be found may be determined in a court of law to be a defense against an infringement claim for a use without permission, there is no guarantee that claiming the work to be an orphan work will be an accepted defense in every case.

Denials

Sometimes a simple "no" comes in reply to a request. Permission may be denied for a variety of reasons. Some authors and owners who have denied our clients' requests for permission to use a quotation are Woody Allen, the estate of Erma Bombeck, Ray Bradbury, and Jane Fonda. See Chapter 11 for a discussion of reasons for denials.

Inaccessibility to Physical Object

If the work you wish to use is in a private collection, you may not be able to obtain a copy of it at a resolution suitable for printing or posting. There may be no public access to the work and thus no way to obtain a copy that is satisfactory for your purposes in publishing. Museums and galleries, for example, disallow any photographing and may or may not sell digital copies. If they do sell copies at an adequate resolution, the fees may not fit in your budget. It is best to determine accessibility and fees before committing much time and energy to including use of such an item in your project plans.

Chapter 11: Reasons for Denials

Some of the reasons permission requests are denied include:

- ✓ Fragmented use of content
- ✓ Primary source not cited in request
- ✓ Misquotations
- ✓ Objectionable content
- ✓ Censorship
- ✓ Unacceptable paraphrasing
- ✓ Need for accessibility to the physical object

Each of these reasons for denial is discussed below.

Fragmented Use of Content

Permission may be denied when content borrowers excerpt phrases from various paragraphs (or possibly from the same paragraph) and string them together. Below is an example of fragmented use of content that may result in denial of permission.

This example is from *To Build a Fire* by Jack London. (This actually is a public domain work, so permission was not needed to paraphrase. It is used to model the kind of paraphrasing a current copyright holder would likely deny.)

Excerpted content that would likely be denied.
He plunged in among the big spruce trees . . . a warm-whiskered man, . . . high cheek-bones. At the man's heels trotted a . . . wolfdog . . . without any temperamental difference from . . . the wild wolf.

Original
He plunged in among the big spruce trees. The trail was faint. A foot of snow had fallen since the last sled had passed over, and he was glad he was without a sled, traveling light. In fact, he carried nothing but the lunch wrapped in the handkerchief. He was surprised, however, at the cold. It certainly was cold, he concluded as he rubbed his numb nose and cheek-bones with his mittened hand. He was a warm-whiskered man, but the hair on his face did not protect the high cheek-bones and the eager nose that thrust itself aggressively into the frosty air.

At the man's heels trotted a dog, a big native husky, the proper wolfdog, gray-coated and without any visible or temperamental difference from its brother, the wild wolf. The animal was depressed by the tremendous cold. It knew that it was no time for traveling. Its instinct told it a truer tale than was told to the man by the man's judgment.

Figure 1: Fragmented use of content

CAUTION: A grant of permission to use a copyrighted work does not mean a permission to change a work unless the permissions agreement states it is acceptable to make changes.

Primary Source Not Cited in Request

Failure to cite the primary source can sometimes result in the rights owner failing to act or denying permission until the original source is cited in a follow-up permission request. A secondary source could be a collection of essays or an anthology, for example.

Also, the mistake of requesting permission from a secondary source when you could have easily located the primary source may result in an unnecessary delay of several weeks, if not several months, in getting your book to press.

TIP: It's wise to locate and use the primary source of the content in order to find the owner or administrator of rights.

If you do not have access to the primary source or know how to locate it, check Chapter 15 for an explanation of how you can often use a secondary source to find the primary source.

Misquotations

Quotations taken from secondary sources such as websites are often inaccurate. Administrators do check borrowed quotes against original words and most likely will deny permission for use of a misquotation. Whenever possible, use the primary source and check the quote carefully to be sure you have copied it correctly.

CAUTION: Misquotations are ubiquitous on the Internet.

Objectionable Content

Permission requests are sometimes denied because the work of the requesting person in some way reflects ideas and/or contains content that the grantor determines to be objectionable. Also, revisions to a textual work or a work of visual art by the copier may be deemed by the original creator of the work to be defamatory, libelous, fraudulent, pornographic, or obscene.

Censorship

Rights owners may consider any alteration of their content to be a form of censorship and may deny permission on this basis. Below is an example of such an alteration. The motivation for changing the words in this instance might be the desire to "clean up" the work in order to meet certain standards set by school boards. Most copyright owners would frown upon the attempt to "clean up" the language with the paraphrasing in the made-up example below. This example is similar to an actual request made by one of our clients that was denied on the grounds of censorship.

EXAMPLE

> The mafia boss walked into the restaurant and saw his rival sitting in his booth.
>
> "What the [heck] are you doing? [Dadgummit] do you want to die? I'll be [darned] if I am going to let you take over the East Side, too. Stay out of my territory or you will have your [ugly] head blown off!"
>
> from *The Family* by Some Author © 2011
> NOTE: Strong language was used in the original. It was replaced by words in brackets.

 CAUTION: An author could ask permission to make modifications to the original text in the original request. However, sending out "trial balloons" in permissions requests will likely consume a lot of time and in many instances will result in a negative response.

Paraphrasing

The example above is an example of paraphrasing as well as an example of censorship. Paraphrasing may be employed to alter sections of works that are considered offensive to the content user. Other reasons for paraphrasing are to mask the use of someone else's content and thus attempt to avoid asking for permission or paying a use fee; to shorten the original item to fit the user's needs in relation to space; and/or to attempt to explain the complicated or complex subject of the copied work to a lay audience.

Paraphrasing is often specifically disallowed in permissions agreements. Permissions agreement terms many times state that no alteration may be made to the original work. Even if no such statement is included in the agreement, if there is no statement specifically allowing it, paraphrasing could precipitate an infringement claim. If you often are tempted to paraphrase the work of others, as an editor I would suggest you ask yourself if the content you are presenting fills a need or if you aren't simply restating what already has been presented in an understandable form. If that is the case, you may want to rethink your treatment of a topic or choose another topic.

 CAUTION: Making assumptions regarding the acceptability or legality of paraphrasing without permission can be risky.

Chapter 12: Locating Contact Information within Various Media

You will need the following information about a work in order to make a permissions request to its owners or administrators: (1) the publisher, (2) where the work was published, (3) the media of the work, (4) the publishing date, (5) the author or the administrator if someone other than the author handles its rights, and (6) the location within the original work of the content you are copying. Below are some helpful hints about where to locate such information in works disseminated in various media.

Print books and ebooks
>
> Check the copyright page for the publisher and/or its copyright owner. Most often, permissions requests go to the publisher of a book.

Periodicals
>
> Check the byline of an article you wish to use if you cannot find information regarding copyright in the front of the periodical. You can also write or email the periodical for copyright ownership information regarding a specific article.

Websites
>
> Look for contact information on the web page containing the content you wish to use. If there is no permissions contact or description with visual art or text, use the contact email or block form on the site to ask about the site's permission procedures.

Audiobooks and CDs
>
> For audiobooks and CDs, check the case cover for information about the publisher and/or copyright owner or administrator.

Visual Art
>
> Photographs, graphic art, and fine art often carry a notice on the page where the item is found. Sometimes all such credits for a particular work can be found on one page near the beginning or end of the publication.

Song Titles
>
> For song titles, check jacket covers, or conduct searches on websites for the US Copyright Office (www.copyright.gov/records/); the American Society of Composers, Authors, and Publishers (ASCAP) (www.ascap.com/); and Broadcast Music, Inc. (BMI) (www.bmi.com/search). Remember, the songwriter usually holds copyright on the lyrics, not the performer—unless the performer is also the writer of the lyrics.

Scan the QR code below to check out a useful ongoing discussion about plagiarism issues on www.PlagiarismToday.com.

Chapter 13: Beyond the Obvious—Where to Look Next

Don't Have Immediate Access to a Copy of the Book?

One method of finding a copyright page for a book you cannot easily access is a feature of Amazon.com that allows the viewer to look inside the book. Not all books allow a look inside, but many do. Chapter 15 shows how to use this feature to quickly see pertinent copyright information regarding text ownership and rights administrators.

You may also find on the copyright page, or possibly on visible pages within the book, a mention of the original source for illustrations, photos, and fine art in the book.

TIP: Before requesting permission, it is important to make sure the administrator (often the publisher) you locate in this manner is actually the administrator for the edition of the work from which you have copied. Ownership and administrators often change, and location of content will vary in different editions.

Nothing Helpful on the Copyright Page?

Check for an acknowledgments page. An acknowledgments page in a secondary source, such as a collection of works or an anthology, will contain valuable leads to the rights owners. As previously stated, in most instances a secondary source will NOT be empowered to grant permission. Secondary sources are those sources that use the words or ideas of others. The acknowledgments page often tells where creators of the secondary work obtained permission to use the original work. In Chapter 15, you will find a detailed discussion of how to make use of an acknowledgments page in a book that is a collection of copyrighted works.

TIP: Check the acknowledgments sections of collective works or other secondary sources for source information about copyrighted works contained therein.

A bibliography is helpful at times in locating the original source for a quotation. It is always best to credit an original source and to seek permission from an original source.

No Helpful Resource Info on the Website?

Sometimes you may find content you wish to use on a website, but can find no credit or acknowledgment. Requests to this website for information about it may go unanswered. This content could be plagiarized. Or the host may own the content or may have permission to publish, but cannot or will not grant that permission to others. If you have relied heavily on this content in creating your own work, you may have a problem down the road.

Finding the original source could be difficult, if not impossible. It's best to prevent such predicaments by determining if the online source is reliable before you commit too much time and too many resources to using it. Your only recourse in a situation where there is a risk of being sued for infringement may be to either scrap your project or spend a great deal of time trying to find the content via web searches using keywords and phrases. If you plan to use content that is taken from websites, before you get too heavily invested in the use, contact the website hosts and see if they can grant permission or guide you to someone who can.

 CAUTION: Much content on the web is plagiarized. Copying content without permission from its copyright owner into a commercial product, such as a book or poster that is to be sold raises the level of risk above what it might be for its use without permission in a noncommercial activity.

 CAUTION: Website creators many times cannot legally grant permission for the copyrighted content on their site.

Other Online Sources

If you cannot find enough publishing information either on an acknowledgments page or a copyright page, try to locate this information at the Library of Congress website (see Appendix A) or by using a combination of online tools such as web searches and Amazon.com to do searches such as those described in Chapter 15.

 TIP: If you cannot locate the information you need or find the search too time consuming using the tools mentioned here, you may want to engage a permissions tracker who has the experience and the knowledge to expedite this kind of search or, if necessary, to engage in a more advanced search.

Chapter 14: Finding the Rights Administrator

Below is a list of various sources that may contain important contact information regarding copyright owners and administrators.

Finding Administrators for a Work within a Collection

If the work you wish to copy comes from a print, audio, or digital collection of works and you cannot find on the copyright page or in the introductory material contact information about individual creators, you should examine its acknowledgments section (see Chapter 15). If the editors of the collective works have acknowledged another source for the work you want to use, you should direct your request to that source.

TIP: When contact information for individual works within a collection isn't in the front matter of the collection or located with each work, check the collection's acknowledgments section.

TIP: If the copyright notice included with an article credits the Associated Press, Reuters, or another news organization, you must direct your permission request to the news agency listed and follow that agency's directions for making a request. For example, the directions for requesting permission from the Associated Press (www.ap.org/company/Terms-conditions) indicate the request must be a written submission.

Finding Administrators for Content in Books and Periodicals

1. Contacts for many publishers can be found in *Literary Market Place*. Your library should have a copy in the reference section. You may also locate publishers online at www.LiteraryMarketPlace.com with a free subscription when you register. This website gives you access to the editorial mailing addresses of US and Canadian publishers, small presses, and international publishers listed by country. Find the publisher on the copyright page in the source you want to use. You can then look it up in Marketplace index.

If the publisher is actually an imprint, the index will provide the name of the parent publisher. It will likely be the parent publisher that will grant permission. Imprints can be thought of as brand names or as marketing mechanisms for different demographics. Publishers use imprints to identify products sold to different markets. An imprint may be one of several trade names owned by a publisher under which a work is published. It can be tricky to track down an imprint without knowledge of the parent company.

For example, the online *Literary Market Place* index shows under its member imprint listing for Alfred A. Knopf that Knopf is one of the many imprints of Random House.

When you know the name of the publisher, you may be able to search online for its official site and find contact information and procedures for requesting permission on the landing page. For example, you can do a web search to find the official Random House website (www.randomhouse.com). At the bottom of the home page under *Services*, there is a link to rights and permissions (www.randomhouse.com/about/permissions.html) that will give you information about requesting permission. This site also has a link to instructions and the permissions form the publisher wants you to use for your request.

2. The Association of American Publishers (AAP) (www.publishers.org/) represents three hundred US publishers of all sizes and types and is a principal trade association in the US book industry. AAP has an index (http://publishers.org/members/) that lists its member publishers under the AAP Members heading.

3. Lists of URLs for information about publishers and imprints may be found on Wikipedia for the following:

- ✓ English-language book publishers (http://en.wikipedia.org/wiki/List_of_English_language_book_publishing_companies)
- ✓ University presses (http://en.wikipedia.org/wiki/List_of_university_presses)
- ✓ UK book publishers (http://en.wikipedia.org/wiki/List_of_largest_UK_book_publishers)

TIP: If you are using copyrighted text or content from a book that is not easily accessible, you could also try a Google search for the word permissions *plus the publisher's name from the copyright page in an Amazon search or in other online searches.*

TIP: If you are quoting from an article in a periodical or newspaper, you may have to contact the publication to find the copyright owner. The contact information or the name of the rights administrator might be located on the copyright page of the periodical, on the page with the article, in a heading above the title, or at the end of the article.

4. Another source for finding copyright owners on the Harry Ransom Center website at the University of Texas at Austin is WATCH (http://norman.hrc.utexas.edu/watch/). This website may be useful in finding copyright information about works from the United Kingdom and has a brief overview of UK copyright laws that differ from US copyright laws.

Finding the Administrator for Online Content

If no copyright information is offered on a website, you may be able to obtain information about the administrator of copyrighted material there by contacting the host of the website. They may be gracious enough to give you information about the original source if they themselves got permission. However, it's important to remember that hosts of sites containing copyrighted content belonging to others cannot themselves, in most cases, grant you permission to use the copied content.

 CAUTION: Website creators most times cannot grant permission for the copyrighted content on their site that was created by others.

Finding Administrators for Artworks or Photographs in Sources Other Than Books

If the artwork or photograph is taken from a book, the information in the previous section will be helpful. Remember, however, that secondary sources such as websites, art texts, and other books that are collections of works many times cannot grant permission to use the works. However, some sites are set up for easy access to administrators of such works.

Art Resource (www.artres.com/C.aspx?VP3=CMS3&VF=ARTHO1_3_VForm) is a good example. Here, you can research fine art images from museums and galleries around the world, request permission for a use, order a digital copy, and make payment for your use online.

For information about support materials requested by administrators, see Chapter 16.

 TIP: For a listing of resources to use in researching photographs and artwork, see Part 4 "Finding and Using Content Created by Others—A List of Resources."

 CAUTION: Copying backgrounds, composition, lighting, etc., from field guides may be infringing. Field guides and reference photos may be intended only as inspiration or as a reference for accuracy.

Finding Administrators for Song Lyrics

You must go to the designated administrator for permission to use song lyrics. Again, it is doubtful that a website or collection containing song lyrics can grant permission for their use.

You can search the website of the American Society of Composers and Publishers (ASCAP) (www.ascap.com/) for song titles to find administrators of rights.

You can also search the website of Broadcast Music, Inc. (BMI) (www.bmi.com/search/) for information about songs and their administrators.

For further information and examples of the process for finding the administrator for song lyrics, see "Song Lyrics" in Part 4: "Finding and Using Content Created by Others—A List of Resources." For a list of support materials that should be included in request packets to be sent to administrators of rights for song lyrics, see Chapter 16.

TIP: Many songs will have more than one owner or administrator. It is wise to give yourself adequate time to secure all needed permissions.

Finding Print Music Publishers

For information about companies that publish printed music, go to directories (www.mpa.org/content/directories) on the Music Publishers Association (MPA) website.

Chapter 15: Secondary Sources to Find Rights Owners

Acknowledgments or Credits Page

When works require several grants of copyright permission, acknowledgments for the grants are often grouped in a special section in the front or back of the book. This section may be titled simply "Credits" or it may be titled "Acknowledgments." The acknowledgments pages that follow in Figure 2 are taken from the book *The Earth Speaks* published by The Institute for Earth Education.

Below is part of the reply to our request to The Institute for Earth Education to use its acknowledgments page as a model to demonstrate how to use a secondary source when tracking down rights administrators.

> "Considering how many times we get requests for material in that book [*The Earth Speaks*] that we don't own the rights to, I think that helping people understand this issue is a great thing."
> (Source: Laurie Farber, International Copyright Coordinator, The Institute for Earth Education)

If you wish to request permission for a work you find in a secondary source, such as in a collection of works like *The Earth Speaks*, you will find its rights administrator in its entry on the acknowledgments page or the credits page of the secondary source.

Note how many of *The Earth Speaks* acknowledgments entries contain the phrase "reprinted by permission of . . . " You will want to contact the rights owners listed following that phrase to obtain permission for the work that the citation references.

CREDITS

We gratefully acknowledge the following authors and publishers for their permission to use their writings in THE EARTH SPEAKS:

A Sense of Place by Alan Gussow. Friends of the Earth.

The Outermost House by Henry Beston. Copyright 1928, 1949, © 1956 by Henry Beston. Copyright © 1977 by Elizabeth C. Beston. Reprinted by permission of Holt, Rinehart and Winston, Publishers.

Sound of Mountain Water by Wallace Stegner. Doubleday and Co.

A Flower Does Not Talk: Zen Essays by Abbot Zenkei Shibayama. Charles E. Tuttle Co., Inc. Japan.

John Burrough's America edited by Farida A. Wiley. Reprinted by permission of The Devin-Adair Co., Old Greenwich, Conn. 06870. Copyright © 1951 by The Devin-Adair Company.

Riprap and Cold Mountain Poems by Gary Snyder. Reprinted by permission of Gary Snyder.

Only A Little Planet by Lawrence Collins. Friends of the Earth.

A Sand County Almanac, with other essays on conservation from Round River by Aldo Leopold. Copyright © 1949, 1953, 1966 renewed 1977, 1981 by Oxford University Press, Inc. Reprinted by permission.

The Great American Forest by Rutherford Platt. Copyright © 1965 by Rutherford Platt. Published by Prentice-Hall, Inc. Englewood Cliffs, NJ 07632.

On the Shred of a Cloud, by Rolf Edberg, translated by Sven Ahman, © 1969, pages 81 and 174. Reprinted by permission of The University of Alabama Press.

Have You Heard the Cricket Song by Winston O. Abbott. Copyright by Winston O. Abbott and Betti Eaton Bosser. Published by Inspiration House.

The Story of My Life by Helen Keller. Grosset & Dunlap, Inc.

Black Elk Speaks by John G. Neihardt. Copyright John G. Neihardt 1932, 1961. Published by Simon & Schuster Pocket Books and the University of Nebraska Press.

Home to the Wilderness by Sally Carrighar. Copyright 1944 by Sally Carrighar. Copyright © 1973 by I.C.E. Limited. Published by Houghton Mifflin Company.

The Seven Mysteries of Life by Guy Murchie. Houghton Mifflin Company. Reprinted by permission of Guy Murchie and Houghton Mifflin Company. © 1978 by Guy Murchie.

"The World's Biggest Membrane" from *The Lives of a Cell: Notes of a Biology Watcher* by Lewis Thomas. Copyright © by the Massachusetts Medical Society. Originally published in the New England Journal of Medicine. Reprinted by permission of Viking Penguin Inc.

Raids on the Unspeakable, by Thomas Merton. Copyright©1965 by the Abbey of Gethsemani, Inc. Reprinted by permission of New Directions, Inc.

Red Salmon Brown Bear by T.J. Walker. Reprinted by permission of the copyright holder.

Canadian Portraits, Brant, Crowfoot, Orohmydtekha, Famous Indians. Ethel Brant Monture. Copyright © 1960 Clark, Irwin, and Co. Ltd., Toronto.

The Way to Start a Day. Copyright Byrd Baylor. Reprinted by permission of the author.

Reflections From the North Country by Sigurd Olson. Copyright © 1976 by Sigurd Olson. Reprinted by permission of Alfred E. Knopf, Inc.

The Immense Journey by Loren Eiseley. Copyright © 1957 by Loren Eiseley. "How Flowers Changed the World" Reprinted by permission of Alfred A. Knopf, Inc.

The Unforeseen Wilderness: An Essay on Kentucky's Red River Gorge. Copyright©1971 Wendell Berry. University Press of Kentucky.

The Sense of Wonder by Rachel Carson. Copyright 1965 by Rachel L. Carson. Reprinted by permission of Harper & Row, Publishers, Inc. Specified exerpt from pp. 42-45.

"The Call of the Wild" from *Collected Poems of Robert Service*. Reprinted by permission of Dodd, Mead and Company, Inc. and The Canadian Publishers, McClelland and Stewart Limited, Toronto.

Fifty-Six from Tao Te Ching by Lao Tsu, translated by Gia-fu Feng and Jane English. Copyright © 1972 by Gia-fu Feng and Jane English. Reprinted by permission of Alfred A. Knopf, Inc.

Northern Farm by Henry Beston. Copyright © 1948 by Elizabeth B. Beston. Reprinted by permission of Holt, Rinehart and Winston, Publishers.

The Prophet by Kahlil Gibran. Copyright © by Kahlil Gibran. Renewal © 1951 by Administrators C.T.A. of Kahlil Gibran Estate, and May G. Gibran. Reprinted by permission of Alfred A. Knopf, Inc.

The Four Seasons. Japanese Haiku, Second Series. Selection by Hokushi. Peter Pauper Press.

Figure 2: Acknowledgments page from *The Earth Speaks*

Used with permission of The Institute for Earth Education

Land of the Spotted Eagle. Chief Luther Standing Bear. Houghton Mifflin Co., 1933.

Songs of the Tewa by Herbert Spinden. AMS Press 1933.

Dune Boy by Edwin Way Teale. © 1943 and 1957 by Edwin Way Teale. Published by Dodd, Mead and Co., New York.

The Little Prince by Saint Exupery. © 1943, 1971 by Harcourt Brace Jovanovich, Inc.

Turtle Island by Gary Snyder. Copyright © 1972, 1974 by Gary Snyder. Reprinted by permission of New Directions.

Pilgrim at Tinker Creek by Annie Dillard. Specified excerpt [Pages 200-201]. Copyright © 1974 by Annie Dillard. Reprinted by permission of Harper and Row, Publishers, Inc.

Seven Arrows by Hyemeyohsts Storm. "Jumping Mouse," pp. 68-85 (text only), Copyright © 1972 by Hyemeyohsts Storm. Reprinted by permission of Harper and Row, Publishers, Inc.

Listening Point by Sigurd Olson. Copyright © 1958 by Sigurd Olson. Reprinted by permission of Alfred A. Knopf, Inc.

"Where the Sidewalk Ends" from *Where the Sidewalk Ends* by Shel Silverstein. Copyright © 1974 by Shel Silverstein. Reprinted by permission of Harper and Row, Publishers, Inc.

Leaves of Grass by Walt Whitman. New American Library.

The Journey Home: Some Words in Defense of the American West. Copyright © 1977 by Edward Abbey. Reprinted by permission of the publisher, E.P. Dutton, Inc.

From *FARMING: A HAND BOOK*, copyright © 1970 by Wendell Berry. Reprinted by permission of Harcourt Brace Jovanovich, Inc.

The Man Who Killed The Deer by Frank Waters. Copyright © 1942, 1970 by Frank Waters. Western Sage (Swallow Press). Reprinted by permission of Joan Daves.

Nature, Man and Women by Alan Watts. Copyright © 1958 by Pantheon Books, a Division of Random House, Inc. Reprinted by permission of the publisher.

Markings by Dag Hammarskjold. Translated by Leif Sjoberg and W.H. Auden. Copyright © 1964 by Alfred A. Knopf, Inc. and Faber and Faber Ltd. Reprinted by permission of Alfred A. Knopf, Inc.

The Desert Year (pp. 4-5 "Why I Came") by Joseph Wood Krutch © 1951, 1952 by Joseph Wood Krutch. Reprinted by permission of William Morrow and Company.

Zen and the Art of Motorcycle Maintenance (Excerpt "Mountains should be climbed...not the top...") by Robert M. Pirsig. Copyright © 1974 by Robert M. Persig. Reprinted by permission of William Morrow and Company.

My First Summer in the Sierra, by John Muir. Copyright renewed 1939 by Wanda Muir Hanna. Reprinted by permission of Houghton Mifflin Company.

The Edge of the Sea, by Rachel Carson. Copyright © 1955 by Rachel L. Carson. Reprinted by permission of Houghton Mifflin Company.

"Earthworm" © 1936, 1964 by Robert Francis. Reprinted from *ROBERT FRANCIS: COLLECTED POEMS 1936-1976* by permission of the University of Massachusetts Press.

© 1961 by John Moffitt. Reprinted from his volume *THE LIVING SEED* by permission of Harcourt Brace Jovanovich, Inc.

The Selected Poetry of Robinson Jeffers. Copyright © 1959 by Robinson Jeffers. Reprinted by permission of Random House, Inc.

NOTE: *Every effort has been made to locate the copyright owners of the materials quoted in the text. Omissions brought to our attention will be credited in subsequent printings.*

Figure 2: Acknowledgments page from *The Earth Speaks* cont.

Used with permission of The Institute for Earth Education

The acknowledgment reference to Sigurd Olson's *Listening Point* underlined in Figure 2 is provided in larger type below.

Listening Point by Sigurd Olson
Copyright © 1958 by Sigurd Olson
Reprinted by permission of Alfred A. Knopf, Inc.

A couple of critical pieces of information are provided in this entry. First, the author holds the copyright, not the publisher. The information that we cannot glean from the entry is the identity of the rights administrator for the author.

To get permission to use a quote from *Listening Point*, for example, you could start by contacting the book's publisher to attempt to find out who controls the rights. In this case, you would begin your permissions tracking by contacting Random House, the parent company of the imprint Alfred A. Knopf, Inc., since that imprint was the administrator who granted the rights to the Institute of Earth Education to publish content from *Listening Point* in *The Earth Speaks*.

This attempt to glean information from the publisher listed in the acknowledgments of an old collection may not give you the answer you are seeking, because the work listed may have changed owners since its publication. If the publisher does not identify the administrator, you may then attempt to find the estate of the author—in this case, that would be Sigurd Olson.

Using Internet Search Tools to Find Sources

We describe below how we used a secondary source to find information on a primary source.

1. We found a copyrighted poem by May Swenson titled "Question" at www.americanpoems.com/poets/May-Swenson/2620.

2. We recorded the URL for this website as a secondary source in the permissions log because the website credits what may be an original source, a book titled *Nature: Poems Old and New* by May Swenson.

3. We then found a copy of *Nature: Poems Old and New* by Googling it. You can see a screenshot of the search results for the title *Nature: Poems Old and New* in Figure 3. The first two entries in Figure 3 show the book at Amazon.com.

NOTE: We feel comfortable using the Google screenshot to demonstrate our process because we have carefully read and followed Google's license regarding such copying. See an explanation of Google's positions on copyright permission in Appendix C.

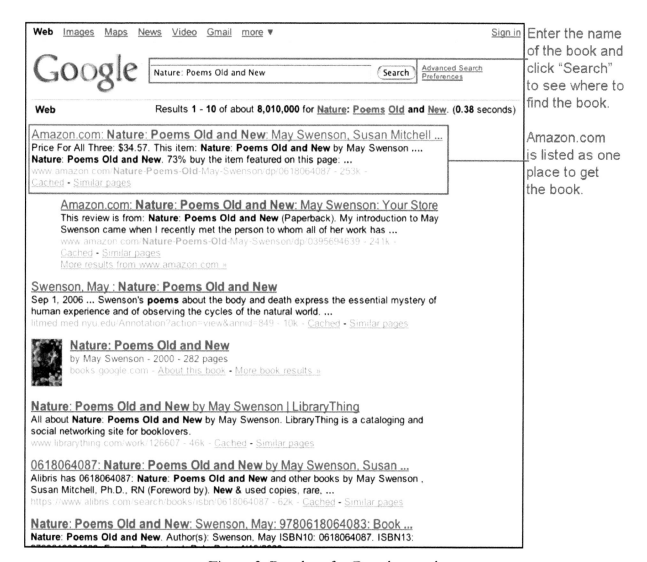

Figure 3: Results of a Google search

4. Click or enter the URL to see the results of the search on the title: www.amazon.com/Nature-Poems-Old-May-Swenson/dp/0618064087.

5. We then used the Amazon.com feature *Search Inside This Book* (a link located below the image of the cover in the left column) to verify the accuracy of content presented in the secondary source.

6. This search feature can be used to look at specific pages, such as the copyright page and index, and to find specific passages, such as the poem "Question," in order to verify accuracy.

7. We clicked on the Copyright Page in the left column. We found it contained several critical items of information that we needed: the imprint is Mariner Books, this book is the 2000 edition, the copyright date is 1994, the Literary Estate of May Swenson holds the rights, and the request for permission must be addressed to Houghton Mifflin Company.

8. We entered the title of the poem, "Question," in the *Search Inside This Book's* search bubble and could see the full poem as published in this source.

Chapter 16: Submitting the Request

Request Formats

There are several ways to make a request for permission: write a letter, fill out an online form, send a fax, or submit the request in an email. See a sample request letter in Appendix D to guide you in making your request. A good example of directions on how to request permission may be found at www.randomhouse.com/about/permissions.html, Random House's website. If you are requesting permission to use text, also see Chapter 8, which lists items contained in permissions agreements for text.

TIP: You can request permission by mail, fax, online forms, or email, depending on the preferences of the administrator.

Faxing the letter and support materials often elicits the quickest response, but some administrators will ask for a hard-copy mailing. Online forms are fast becoming the modus operandi for requesting from most large publishers. Remember to log in all names, dates, and times of communications as you attempt to contact administrators. And don't be surprised if after six to eight weeks with no reply, you contact the administrator again and are told your request cannot be located.

TIP: Keep a record of names of all those contacted and the dates and times contacts are made. Refer to them when you must make a repeat contact. This practice may encourage prompt attention to locating your request or willingness to act quickly on a new request.

CAUTION: Electronic rights may be administered by some entity other than the print rights administrator. It may take several weeks before the print rights administrator directs you to the person to contact for electronic rights. Remember to allow extra time in your acquisition schedule for such a scenario.

Support Materials

If your use consists of copying into a print work, ebook, or course management system, you may be required to send a photocopy or digital file of the pages in your work containing the copied material, as well as the pages in your work located before and after those pages. That way, the administrators can see your use of their work in context.

TIP: More and more publishers are using online forms that do not mention including these support materials but will often request, in a reply after the forms have been submitted online, that these support items be emailed as an attachment or that physical copies be sent by regular mail.

Information Required When Requesting Permission for Various Formats

Include the following items when requesting permission for various formats:

- ✓ Title of your work
- ✓ Author(s) or coauthor(s) of your work
- ✓ Publisher of your work
- ✓ Format of your work (print or digital as in CDs, websites, blogs, ebooks, or course management systems like Blackboard)
- ✓ Specifics of your use (adapt an article by shortening, for example)
- ✓ Territory
- ✓ Number of copies you will print
- ✓ Time frame of your use
- ✓ Information regarding security of use if electronic rights are requested (such as noting that the website will be password protected and made available to a specified number of students)

Information Required about Your Website Use

If you are requesting permission from a print source or digital source (ebooks, blogs, websites, PDFs, course management systems) to place its content on your website, include the following information about your use.

- ✓ The URL of the website
- ✓ The estimated date of your posting
- ✓ Description of your site as either commercial or noncommercial (if it has banner ads or if it is selling product or service directly)
- ✓ The number of visitors or hits you have per day or month
- ✓ The name of the host of your site
- ✓ The length of time you plan to display your work containing the copied work, if your use is on a website
- ✓ The description or example of your planned use
- ✓ Any pertinent information about the security of your site (Is it a password-protected site? A members-only site? Will certain content be watermarked?)

Request to Use Work Found in a Book

It is essential that you locate the primary source of the content you wish to use in your work. The rights administrator of a secondary work containing someone else's content will most likely not be able to grant permission to use the originator's content. Include the following items in your request to use work found in a book:

- ✓ Author of source book
- ✓ Publisher (or imprint) of source book
- ✓ Date the source book was published
- ✓ Copyright date for source book
- ✓ ISBN for source book
- ✓ Number of words you are requesting and page numbers in the source book where the copyrighted content is located

Request to Use Work Found in a Periodical

Include the following items in your request for content from either an online or print periodical:

- ✓ Publication name of periodical
- ✓ Article title and author
- ✓ Section in periodical, if applicable
- ✓ Issue date of periodical
- ✓ Page numbers in periodical or URL from which content to be copied is taken
- ✓ Type of use for this permissions/licensing request (republishing)
- ✓ Detailed information on how the content will be used (Follow instructions and include descriptive items given in this chapter that note your specific use of the periodical content for each format: online use, print use, ebook use, and course management system use.)

An example of an online request form for a periodical can be found at www.nytreprints.com/permissions-licensing-quote-request/.

Request to Use Work Found on a Website

Instructions for requesting work found on a website are given below.

- ✓ Follow contact instructions on the website that contains any copyrighted text, photographs, graphic or fine art, maps, charts, etc., you want to copy.
- ✓ Include the URL and the date the content was first published, if listed, and the date you viewed it on the site. This information will help the owner/administrator locate the content you wish to use.

- ✓ Include the title of the work or a description of the content to be copied if there is no title.
- ✓ Include information about your print work or ebook listed in the previous section titled "Information Required when Requesting Permission for Various Formats" if you plan to print or publish the borrowed content in an ebook.
- ✓ Tell the rights administrator whether the content will be placed on the home page or an internal page on your website.
- ✓ Give the name of the creator of the source content (writer, photographer, artist, poet, etc.).
- ✓ Include the following information if you wish to reproduce the copied content onto your website, as it will likely be requested:

  - the URL where the content is to be located on your site
  - the date of posting
  - the length of time the work will be posted
  - the average number of hits per month, if known
  - whether the site is commercial or noncommercial

- ✓ Ask for a warranty that the grantor is the owner of the content or is empowered by the owner to grant permission.

 CAUTION: Because so much content on the Internet is plagiarized or is a secondary source that can contain misquotes, misrepresentations, and infringements, it is important to include a question regarding ownership in your request for permission for Internet content.

Request to a Gallery or Museum

A request to use fine art from a museum or gallery should include the following:

- ✓ Your name
- ✓ The title, creator, and cataloging number, if there is one, of the work requested
- ✓ The required image format (digital, transparency, or slide)
- ✓ Your shipping and billing addresses
- ✓ Your timeline

 CAUTION: There is no way of knowing in a specific case whether a court will decide a use of copyrighted content in a collage is a fair use. If you or your illustrator is combining portions of copyrighted images to create a new image, your use may be considered by a court to be a derivative of several works and therefore copyright infringement.

Request for Use of Song Lyrics

If the use consists of song lyrics, include the following items with your request:

- ✓ The title of the song
- ✓ The name(s) of the songwriter(s)
- ✓ A photocopy of the title and the copyright notice on the DVD cover and/or of the text inside the package (This is not always required but may be helpful in some cases.)
- ✓ An acknowledgment of lyric ownership by another publisher/writer if more than one is listed on the cover (You will likely need to make a request to all owners or their administrators. This may require submitting several separate requests.)

TIP: If you are able to make a request using contact information found on the websites of ASCAP and BMI, remember to look for a listing there of all writers and publishers and to request all necessary permissions.

Request Work Form

Figures 4 and 5 below represent Parts A and B of a request work form that identifies the information typically needed when making a request to use content from someone else's book. Part A identifies the source of the text that you want permission to use in your book. Part B describes your book and publication projections in some detail.

You may adapt the form for the kind of source you are using, relying on the information that has been given in this chapter.

The full Excel version of the form, including notes on various items, is available online at www.TheCopyrightDetective.com/guide/WorkForm.

Request Work Form

Sample work form for making a request when copying from a book. You may adapt the form for the kind of source you are using, relying on the information presented in the workbook.

PART A: THEIR BOOK

Title of book: [   ]

Subtitle: [   ]

ISBN: [   ]

Publication date: [   ]

Total number of words you wish to use: [   ]

Total page count in book: [   ]

Copyright line from book: [   ]

Page numbers where copied work is located: [   ]

Publisher: [   ]

Imprint: [   ]

Location of publisher: [   ]

Names/Numbers of Illustrations: [   ]

Total number of illustrations: [   ]

Credit line for illustrations: [   ]
[If copyright holder is other than your source, you may need their permission.]

Figure 4: Request Work Form, Part A

PART B: YOUR BOOK

Territories where book will be distributed:

Types/Formats:

Security for content:

Book title:

Subtitle:

Number of pages:

Author(s) name(s):

Publisher:

	Date of Publication	Copies, Views, or Downloads	Retail Price	ISBN
Trade paper				
Hardcover				
eBook				
Online				
Other digital				
Audio				

Course management system:

Number of students accessing:

Time frame for use:

Duration of request for print versions:

Duration of request for digital/website:

Languages in which printed:

Describe alterations/modifications to the copyrighted content:

Format to be used to credit the granted work:

Rights requested:

Nature of the book, website:

Description of the book, website, ebook, audio book:

Figure 5: Request Work Form, Part B

Scan the QR code below to access the Excel work request forms shown above. The password may be acquired by registering the purchase of the book. Registration is required only once to receive the passwords for all the restricted online resources.

Chapter 17: Follow-Up Activities

Copyright Management Information

Remember to enter data regarding the initial request in your permissions log. See Appendix H for templates of permissions logs for works in various formats. Before exiting permission request sites, remember to download and print and/or save copies of the completed online request forms in designated folders. It's important to keep track of dates and contacts for all requests.

Status of Requests

If you have not received an answer from rights administrators when their "normal processing time" has elapsed, phone them or send an email asking for the status of your request. It will be helpful to have the information about your requests in front of you when you do the follow-up. They often will ask for the date you sent the first request and the dates you sent any follow-up requests.

Enter data regarding your follow-up requests in your permissions log regarding when and who you contacted, how you contacted them, when you received any replies, and the content of the reply.

If you are not getting any response, you may attempt to locate another administrator, since works often change ownership. If your first choice of administrators or rights owners turns out be incorrect, other administrators may guide you to the right one. Or you may have to do some detective work. Sometimes, you have to contact several publishers and an estate or an agency before locating the correct owner or administrator of the rights.

Enter data in your permissions log regarding any second and subsequent requests.

License Analysis and Compliance

A sample grant letter agreement may be seen in Appendix E.

When you do receive the license or letter of agreement, read it carefully for details regarding your obligations and the limitations it places on your use. Some items to look for in an agreement follow:

- the fees for print use and for electronic use (ebooks)

71

- language similar to most favored nations clause
- the number of copies in which you are allowed to include the content
- the number of copies (if any) the grantor requests of your book
- the date by which you must send payment and copies of your book
- how they want their credit to read in your book, and if they stipulate placement and formatting requirements for the credit

Enter data regarding the license in your permissions log: all the information cited in the agreement, the date it was received, the fee, and who sent the agreement.

Formatting credits

Format credits on the acknowledgments or copyright page if your work is to be available in print and/or ebook formats. If your use is to be an online use, put the credits on the page where copyrighted content is located. In planning formatting for credits, remember to consider the administrators' stipulations regarding their content and format. You can usually allow yourself some leeway in formatting credits in regards to style choices. However, an agreement might actually stipulate that variation from a specific credit line voids the agreement. Check your credits against the agreement requirements.

For a visual work such as an illustration or photograph, the agreement may stipulate that the credit listed be with the work. You may be required to put the title and creator's name in close proximity to the work as well as put a permission acknowledgment on the copyright page.

Complimentary copies

At the appropriate time, mail out the specified number of copies of your book to those publishers whose licenses stipulate they are to receive copies. Many publishers will ask for two copies. They may check your publication to see if your use of their content complies with the license agreement.

Monitor copies distributed

When you go into a second printing (and supplemental printings), check your permissions log to see if you have printed the maximum number of copies allowed by your license and if you need to renew your license to allow for more copies. If you are using a print on demand (POD) printing service, monitor the total number of books printed. If your work is online, check the time frame you were allowed by your permissions agreement and remove content when time has elapsed or request permission for extended time. For ebooks, monitor sales from all distributors, including those to libraries and those from your own website, if applicable.

Chapter 18: Steps in the Permissions Process

Text

1. As you work on your manuscript, compile all the copyright information for any items you may wish to use, so that you can easily locate them again.
2. Compile all the information about your work necessary for making permission requests.
3. Locate the copyright owners.
4. Send letters or fill out online forms to request permission.
5. Negotiate fees if administrators' processes allow for it.
6. Get a signed permissions agreement from the owners of the copyrighted works.
7. Get warranties that the administrators have the right to grant you the rights to use the works.
8. Enter all information into your log.
9. Be sure you adhere to all stipulations in the agreements such as those regarding sending copies and paying fees.

Images

1. Compile information on all the images you may wish to use.
2. Acquire royalty-free and public domain images, and check alternative licensed images or commissioned images.
3. Secure a signed agreement or purchase a license for royalty-free images granting permission for images that are not public domain and for uses that you determine cannot be claimed as fair use.
4. Secure a signed agreement that clearly defines ownership for any commissioned works.

CAUTION: Be aware that what has been deemed a "commissioned work" may not fall into one of the nine categories required for a "work made for hire" classification. Whether you are a commissioner of a work or one who is commissioned to do a "work made for hire," you may want to research differing opinions from the artist's perspective, the author's perspective, and from the publisher's perspectives on "work made for hire" before you sign any "work made for hire" agreements. You also may want to research opinions held by the Graphic Artist Guild, the American Society for Journalists and Authors (ASJA) and the Independent Book Publishers Association (IBPA). And/or you may want to hire an attorney to help with this kind of agreement. You will want to be clear on who owns the copyright for the images BEFORE you publish your work.

5. Make sure you file electronic and print copies of each agreement, including any click wrap licenses and any Creative Commons licenses.
6. Enter all the information in your permissions tracking logs.
7. Be sure you adhere to all stipulations in the licenses and permissions agreements, such as those regarding giving credits, sending copies, and making payments.

PART 4: FINDING AND USING CONTENT CREATED BY OTHERS–A LIST OF SOURCES

Library of Congress

You can search the Library of Congress's (LOC) vast collections of prints and photographs at its website www.loc.gov/pictures/. For example, there is a collection of 2,100 images of baseball cards dating from 1887 to 1914. Many of the millions of images are accompanied by information about their rights status. Appendix A shows screenshots that may help you understand procedures used in LOC searches.

The American Memories collections on topics such as historic maps, Native American history, African American history, immigration, and the environment include images and photographs, as well as audio and video digital resources. For more links and detailed information about copyrights for items in this collection, go to http://memory.loc.gov/ammem/awhhtml/awamdigres.html.

 CAUTION: Don't assume that everything on the LOC website is public domain because some copyright-restricted items are included. And sometimes no rights information is provided for an item on the LOC website. In that case, you should assess the risk of using the image.

The website www.loc.gov/rr/print/195_copr.html#catalog explains the use of rights information attached to images. The thorough discussion and explanation should help you decide what to do about using an LOC image. And you can find an example of a rights statement about an LOC image at www.loc.gov/rr/print/res/079_vanv.html.

Smithsonian

You can search the Smithsonian Institution Archives for images held by the Smithsonian. Be aware that this site carries a warning: "All photographs copyright Smithsonian Institution. Do not reproduce without written permission." The Smithsonian Institute website (http://siarchives.si.edu/services/rights-and-reproduction) provides information about obtaining permission to use photographs.

New York Times

The *New York Times* provides an online form to request permission for text use. To obtain permission to use *New York Times* photographs, charts, maps, and other graphic elements, contact Redux Pictures at (212) 253-0399. More info about obtaining various permissions, such as permission to use a screen grab, can be found on the *New York Times* website. (Source: www.nytimes.com/content/help/rights/permissions/permissions.html)

Association of American University Presses

For a directory of nonprofit and independent publishers of fiction and nonfiction educational materials, textbooks, supplements, and so forth, go to the Association of American University Presses (AAUP) website. (Source: www.aaupnet.org/policy-areas/copyright-a-access/copyright-a-permissions/copyright-a-permissions/permissions-information-directory)

Columbia University

A database of international copyright law is provided on Columbia University's website (http://digital.lampdev.columbia.edu/cmc/). The site also has an interesting feature that allows you to compare up to three criteria for three countries simultaneously. (Source: http://digital.lampdev.columbia.edu/cmc/index.php/compare/compare)

Associated Press

To acquire permission to use Associated Press (AP) articles and images, and to acquire digital images from this news-gathering agency—which offers one of the world's largest collections of historical and contemporary imagery—go to the Associated Press website (www.ap.org). You'll find a block form to request permission to use their content. (Source: www.ap.org/products-services/contact/permissions)

The Commons on Flickr

This image and video hosting site offers access to many images from institutions such as libraries and historical societies, as well as government entities. Be sure to read item 2 in Chapter 4 as well as rights information on The Commons on the Flickr website regarding restriction language, before determining which images you will publish. (Source: www.flickr.com/commons/usage/)

Project Gutenberg

Project Gutenberg is book digitization project that offers 40,000 public domain titles for download in ebook formats. The website also provides a "self-publishing portal" with more than 100,000 ebook titles that have been made available for free public access. (Source: www.gutenberg.org)

 CAUTION: Before republishing titles of public domain books you find on the project site with their trademark attached, read the Gutenberg license agreement for limitations on your use. You may wish to strip the Gutenberg project trademark from the public domain works found here so

that you may make modifications to it and so that you do not have to pay a royalty to the project for each sale.
(Source: www.gutenberg.org/wiki/Gutenberg:The_Project_Gutenberg_License)

Other Sources for Photographs and Images

US Government Photos and Images

The US government has thousands of images and photographs on various websites, and many of them are in the public domain and may be used without restriction. The www.usa.gov/Topics/Graphics.shtml website provides a portal into eight major categories of images, such as "Defense and International Relations," which has ten sections under it, including the various branches of the Armed Forces. The US Air Force section has thirty-two subcategories, including topics you wouldn't expect such as "Colorado Wildfire."

The National Archives is another excellent source of public domain images. One of the tools on the website is the Archival Research Catalog (ARC), which contains numerous galleries of photographs, images, graphics, maps, and so on. (Source: www.archives.gov/research/arc/)

 CAUTION: Some of these photos and images posted on US government websites are in the public domain and may be used and reproduced without permission or fee. However, some photos and images may be protected by license. We strongly recommend you thoroughly read the disclaimers on each site before use.

National Geographic

National Geographic offers two kinds of images and photographs: royalty free and rights managed. See the definitions of these terms in the Glossary. Be aware that *royalty free* does not mean you may use an image without paying for it.
(Source: www.nationalgeographicstock.com/ngsimages/welcome.jsf)

Stock Photography

- Dreamstime (www.dreamstime.com)

- Fotolia (http://us.fotolia.com)

- Fotosearch (www.fotosearch.com)

- Getty Images (www.gettyimages.com/Creative/Frontdoor/PhotoDisc)

- iStockphoto (www.istockphoto.com)

- Jupiterimages (www.jupiterimages.com)

- MorgueFile (http://morguefile.com)

- Shutterstock (www.shutterstock.com)

- Stock.XCHNG (www.sxc.hu)

- Thinkstock (www.thinkstockphotos.com/photostogo)

Image Banks/Famous People

- Culver Pictures (www.culverpictures.com/about.html)

- Everette Collection (www.everettcollection.com)

- Time & Life Pictures (www.timelifepictures.com/ms_timepix/source/home/home.aspx?pg=1)

- Corbis Images (www.corbisimages.com)

- Digital Collections and Services, Library of Congress: Choose the topic Prints and Photographs and click on the link about PPOC for information about ordering digital images. (www.loc.gov/pictures/)

Cartoons

Cartoons can be republished to inform and enliven blogs, newsletters, books, and presentations. Below are some good resources for copyrighted cartoons.

- Collections of cartoon drawings, Library of Congress: Some cartoons remain under copyright, such as those of political cartoonist Herbert L. Block, which are held by the Herb Block Foundation. (www.loc.gov/rr/print/res/271_herb.html)

- Association of American Editorial Cartoonists (AAEC) (http://editorialcartoonists.com)

- National Cartoonists Society (www.reuben.org/news/)

- Daryl Cagle's PoliticalCartoons.com (www.politicalcartoons.com)

- Harpers Weekly: Historical cartoons from old issues (www.harpweek.com)

- The Cartoon Bank, Condé Nast: Cartoons from *The New Yorker* magazine (www.cartoonbank.com/License/page/cblicense)

- Universal Uclick (www.universaluclick.com/comics)

Fine and Graphic Art Images

AIGA, the Professional Association for Design: AIGA features member portfolios. (http://portfolios.aiga.org)

American Society of Architectural Illustrators (ASAI) (www.asai.org)

Art Resource: You can search this site for more than 500,000 fine art images. This is one of the best sources for artwork for your publication. Art Resource has a helpful staff and easy search mechanism. A fee is charged for use, but not for help in locating your artist or image, if you are having trouble with a search of the site. (www.artres.com)

Artists Rights Society: This organization grants permission for the use of many works of art. The website provides helpful information about clearing rights. (www.arsny.com)

Corbis Images: Corbis Images offers collections of royalty free and rights managed images for commercial and editorial use. See the Glossary for definitions of these terms. (www.corbisimages.com)

For less well-known artists, try the gallery or institution in which the artist's work is exhibited. Google searches of names or titles of works may help, too.

Dover Publications: This company publishes books featuring public domain art. (http://store.doverpublications.com/index.html)

 CAUTION: *Always check licenses or details about the use of any images. Many Dover images, for example, are public domain, and the company makes clear that anyone may use up to a certain percentage of these in any one product. But take care not to copy a larger portion of the collection than they allow, as they claim copyright on the collection as a whole.*

Getty Images: Getty Images provides access to creative imagery, music, and video content. See the rights and clearance section for details. (www.gettyimages.com)

Graphic Artist Guild: The Guild is an advocacy group for creative professionals. (www.graphicartistsguild.org)

Time & Life Pictures: Digital Time & Life images are available through Getty Images. (www.timelifepictures.com/ms_timepix/source/home/home.aspx?pg=1)

VAGA: VAGA is an artists' rights organization and copyright collective that represents reproduction rights for thousands of artists worldwide. (www.vagarights.com)

 TIP: Google Images may be a good place to start searching for images on a specific topic. But always seek permission on these images, unless they are under a Creative Commons license that allows the use you wish to make of the image or they are in the public domain.

Song Lyrics

Search the site for the American Society of Composers and Publishers (ASCAP) for song titles, songwriters, and publishers to find administrators of rights. ASCAP does not administer the rights to copy lyrics, but it is invaluable in helping to identify who does. Start the process by searching the ACE database. If all the rights holders to a song are not ASCAP members, the database often will point to the entity that does administer the rights. (www.ascap.com/Home/ace-title-search/index.aspx)

You may also search the website of Broadcast Music, Inc. (BMI) for information about 7.5 million musical works and their administrators. Start by putting in information about the work in the "Search the Repertoire" section. The first thing that happens is you will get a click agreement stating you understand the terms of the site. Once you click Accept, you will be able to view the database. The database may display multiple variations of the same title. Make sure you are pursuing the correct work before contacting the publisher. (www.bmi.com/search/)

Fotolia.com is one of the many sources of royalty-free graphics and photographs that can be used to illustrate books, websites, marketing materials, and so on. To see an example, scan the QR code below to access the web page for the "Helpful Tips" graphic used in this book.

PART 5: PROTECTING YOUR WORK AGAINST ABUSE

The Electronic Copyright Office (eCO) is the preferred way to register a copyright. Scan the QR code below to access the website. It is recommended that you view the tutorials at the top of the web page before starting the process. It isn't rocket science, but it does take patience and persistence to go through the many steps in the process.

Chapter 19: Registering Your Work

Why Register?

A work is copyrighted from the time it is created in a tangible form. So why go to the trouble to register it?

Federal registration in a timely manner has several advantages. Creators must register their copyright in order to bring an infringement lawsuit in a U.S. court. Registration of a work establishes a date of publication for it and makes it a matter of public record. If the creators wait until there is an infringement of their work before they register the copyright, they either may have to wait four months or more to receive the certificate necessary to bring suit, or they may have to pay a substantial fee to expedite registration in order speed up the processing.

Also, the creator of a work who wins a suit, but has not registered the copyright within *three months* of the work's publication date, may not be entitled to receive statutory damages or have legal costs and attorney's fees paid by the infringer. The winner in such a suit may instead receive what the court considers actual damages. An award of actual damages would likely mean receiving much less money than would have been awarded had the work been registered during the three-month period.

 CAUTION: Remember, it is a myth that creators can mail themselves a copy of their work and successfully use this mailing as established proof of ownership when making an infringement claim. Such a mailing likely would not be considered proof of ownership in a court of law.

Registration Procedures

The US Copyright Office provides the online form eCO, which may be used to register a single work, a collection of unpublished works by the same author and owned by the same claimant, or multiple published works in the same unit of publication owned by the same claimant. Form eCO may be found by clicking the How to Register a Work option on the main website. There you will find links to a number of tutorials and references such as eCo tips, eCo FAQs, an eCo tutorial, and eCo updates. The tutorial contains step-by-step instructions, with screenshots and detailed explanations. (www.copyright.gov/eco/)

When to Register Your Work

For text, visual art, print, or digital works—including blogs, newsletters, and ebooks—a registered copyright may be obtained after you have completed the work in tangible form.

Date of Publication versus Publication Date

The "date of publication" requested on the copyright registration form can be (1) the date your work came off the press, (2) the shipping date, or (3) the publication date. The "publication date" is the official date your work is released to the public. It's the date you expect to publicize availability in your media releases.

If your book comes off the press at the end of the year, it is usually a good idea to give it a copyright date of January of the following year so it won't appear to be a year-old publication to reviewers and book buyers. You would put the January date on the copyright registration form as the date of publication, in that case.

Date of Publication for Online Works

You can register your web pages with the US Copyright Office. The date of publication for online works is the date the works were first displayed.

Length of Return Time for Registration Notification

Online registration promises a quicker return than a mail-in registration, which ordinarily can take six months or more. At the time of this writing, the Copyright Office is reporting an average time of two and a half months for processing e-filings. However, the issuing of some registration notifications is now taking eighteen months or more. The effective date of registration, however, is the date the Copyright Office receives the application if the application meets all procedural and legal requirements.

Copyright Protection of Works

Your book is protected from the moment you create it in tangible form. However, you cannot sue in federal court until your work is registered with the US Copyright Office.

The registration fee using the eCO online application process is $35 for a basic claim. If you print out the registration form and return it via mail—or fill out a form you have requested via mail and returned it via mail—you will be charged $65. Always check the instruction circulars and the US Copyright Office website for fees and current processing times for the latest changes. (www.copyright.gov/help/faq/faq-what.html#certificate)

Chapter 20: Taking a Proactive Approach

You should know not only how copyright clearance and licensing affects your use of others' works, but also how it affects how others may use your works. Protect your own work against content theft.

Make Your Use Rules Obvious

If you are willing to let others use some of your work in some cases, give potential users clear instructions about exactly how they may use your work and where and how to request permission, if a request is something you require. Put that information in an obvious and easily accessible place on your work.

> Example
> For permission to use any portion of the content in this book (or on this website, article, or other source), send your request to _____. *(Provide your mailing address, email address, or link.)*

If you wish to share some content freely in certain situations, use the appropriate Creative Commons (CC) symbols for any sections you wish to share. This frees you from having to answer permission requests on certain uses. Before you decide to share your work in this way, make sure you read Appendix F about considerations for such a use. And if you do choose to share through a Creative Commons license, make sure you use the correct symbol denoting the limitations on the way you are sharing the work.

Give Notice of Your Ownership

If your work is in a print or digital format, make sure it contains a formal copyright notice. Before 1978, US copyright law required a copyright notice be placed on a work for it to be copyright protected. A copyright notice was not required by law for works published between 1978 and 1989 in the US if the work was registered within five years of its publication. Since 1989 US copyright law has not required a written copyright notice, regardless of the existence of federal registration.

However, placing a copyright notice on any work you want protected is a good practice because it deters infringers. It also makes it easier to prove that an infringing party did so willfully. Having a copyright notice on the work makes it difficult for people to successfully claim they didn't know your work was copyrighted. Courts often award far higher amounts in statutory damages where infringement can be shown to be willful.

Monitor Others' Uses of Your Work

Require a Copy of the Requestor's Completed Work

If you grant permission to use your work, include in the agreement the requirement that you be provided with a copy of the new work. When you receive it, check to see if the use is what you allowed.

Plagiarism Checkers for Images

If your work is online, you may wish to search for unauthorized use of your images. There are tools online to help with such searches, including the choices listed below.

TinEye.com

TinEye is a reverse image search engine that finds copies of an image on the Internet, tells you where it came from, how it is being used, if modified versions of the image exists, and if there is a higher resolution version somewhere. (www.tineye.com)

Google Image Search

Google now has a feature called Search by Image, which allows you to search for infringing pictures. Just drag the image into the search box, and the service will locate any instances on the web where that image occurs.
(www.google.com/insidesearch/features/images/searchbyimage.html)

Who stole my pictures

Who stole my pictures is a Mozilla Firefox extension that expedites a search of several image search engines, including Tineye.com, Yandex-ru (a popular Russian search engine), Google.com, Baidu.com (a Chinese web services company), and Cydral.com (a search add-on for Google Chrome). You can simply go to the Who stole my pictures site, and from there, with a click of the mouse, move to any of these sites. (https://addons.mozilla.org/en-US/firefox/addon/who-stole-my-pictures/)

 CAUTION: Images are infringed upon more than any other kind of content on the web. In order to protect your work, use digital watermarks on your visual art (photographs, maps, illustrations, fine art, graphic art).

Plagiarism Checkers for Text

If your work is online, you may wish to search for phrases and single lines from inside your document since an infringer can easily change titles and headings. There are online tools to help with tracking text content on the Internet, including Copyscape.com, Google Alerts (www.google.com/alerts), and Plagium (www.plagium.com) for up to 25,000 characters.

 TIP: New products and methods of detection will likely present themselves often, so always check for the latest. Research comparisons for the best fit for your detections needs.

Secure and Understand Agreements, Licenses, and Grants

Get all permissions and license agreements in writing. With only a verbal agreement, a misunderstanding between you and a requester or coworker on a project may put a damper on your project or halt completion altogether. One of our clients, a children's book author and independent publisher, had a verbal agreement with an illustrator. They had originally decided they would split any royalties. The illustrator later decided she wanted payment up front after much of the work had been completed and many discussions about its use had taken place. The author's budget didn't allow for such a change of heart. This created a snag in the publishing process that placed a dark cloud over this project and plans for future books in the series.

Remember to clarify in your permissions agreements what rights you are allowing. Some rights already mentioned in this book are electronic rights, exclusive and nonexclusive rights, rights to use in works only for specific territories, and rights to use in works only in specified languages. If you charge a fee for permission to use your work, you should consider the value of the use under each of the rights included in your license before setting a permissions fee in your agreement. You may also wish to specify the length of time your work may be used, and limit the use to a specific work title, number of copies, number of users, and format.

 CAUTION: If you are an artist doing a commissioned work, remember that signing a "work made for hire" agreement can mean you lose all rights forever. If you are an author commissioning an artist to create what you consider to be a "work made for hire" for you, or you are creating what you consider to be a "work made for hire," remember that not all work falls into one of the nine categories of a "work made for hire" in US copyright law. If the circumstances under which the work is done do not fit the legal requirement for a "work made for hire," your agreement may not be binding. The US Copyright Office's Circular 09 explains "work made for hire" under the 1976 Copyright Act. (www.copyright.gov/circs/circ09.pdf)

Take Action Against Infringers

If the infringer does not have permission to use your work, or if that person was granted limited rights but has used your work in a way you didn't intend or license, you could choose to discuss with this person ways to resolve the situation. If the situation cannot be resolved amicably, you may demand that the works containing your infringed work immediately be taken off display and out of distribution.

If the infringing work is a print work and you consider the infraction great enough to warrant a formal complaint to the infringing party—or legal action—you may choose to first send a cease and desist letter by certified mail. Depending on the severity of the infraction, it may be wise to consider consulting an attorney before you take any action.

Issue a DMCA Takedown Notice

The Digital Millennium Copyright Act (DMCA) is the US copyright law passed in 1998 that provides a notice-and-takedown system to help victims of infringement get offending works removed from the Internet. It offers protection from liability to Internet service providers (ISPs) who follow the procedures set forth in the law. If an ISP receives a takedown notice, as defined by the law, and does not act upon the notice, it may be held liable for the infringement addressed in the notice. (www.copyright.gov/legislation/dmca.pdf)

If an infringement of your work occurs online, you may wish to first send a cease and desist letter (see sample below) to the infringer. If that doesn't get results, you may decide to send a DMCA notification to the web host or ISP.

ISPs are required to make their agent's name and address available to the public. You can find the ISP of the infringing site at www.whois.net/ or www.domaintools.com/.

Items All DMCA Takedown Notices Should Contain

1. The name, address, and signature of the complaining party
2. A statement identifying the work or materials that have been infringed
3. The infringing materials and their Internet locations
4. Enough information to allow the Internet service provider to identify the infringing materials
5. A statement that the owner of the materials has a good faith belief that there is no legal basis to allow the use of the infringing materials
6. A statement of the accuracy of the complaint and that the complaining party has the copyright owner's authorization to be filing the complaint

There is a directory of service provider agents for notification of claims of infringement at www.copyright.gov/onlinesp/list/a_agents.html. If you want to engage someone else to file a takedown notice for you, locate one of the services that will do this for a fee. The site for one of them is located at www.copybyte.com.

Sample Cease and Desist Letter to an Online Infringer

The following is a sample Cease and Desist Letter to a listed registrant contact of an infringing website.

August 21, 2012

Dear Mr. Jones,

It has come to my attention that you have published excerpts from my copyrighted content, an article titled "Going It Alone" (My Work), on your website without my permission. I have reserved all rights in the work and have registered this work with the United States Copyright Office. It was first published in the July 2009 issue of the periodical *Take Courage*. Your work, the blog *Single and Liking It*, located at www.likingit.com, has infringed on my work, reproducing at least four lengthy passages word for word.

I believe you have willfully infringed my rights under 17 U.S.C Section 101 et seq and could be held liable for damages. These damages could be as high as $150,000 as set forth in Section 504 (c) (2) therein.

I demand that you cease the use of My Work on your site. If you have not removed said content within 72 hours, I shall take further actions against you.

Sincerely,
John Smith

The following is a sample Cease and Desist Letter to a print publisher of an infringing work.

May 1, 2012

James Byrd, Owner
Unprincipled Press
Bookerton, OH 43201

Dear Mr. Byrd,

I have discovered an infringement of my work in a book published by Unprincipled Press titled *Pots and Plants* by Josephine Browne.

Enclosed are copies of three illustrations created by me and published in my book titled *Around the Maypole*.

I demand that you cease and desist from selling or distributing any copies of *Pots and Plants*. I also demand that you compensate me for use of my work.

Please respond to this cease and desist letter by June 3, 2012.

Sincerely,
Jim Trueman

Cc: Josephine Browne
    220 Listview Circle
    Omaha, NE 80023

Model Takedown Notice

The following is a sample takedown notice that would be sent to an ISP hosting company that is hosting an infringing website.

Send to: dmca@gracious.connect.net (example email address of ISP)

TO: Gracious Connect Hosting (name of the ISP Hosting Company):
FROM: Armond Ruin (your name)
RE: A Copyright Claim

I am writing to inform you that the illustrations at the URL below are infringing my copyright. I have attached copies of the illustrations to help you locate the infringing material.

(List the URL or URLs where infringement is located.)

This is an official notification under the provisions set down in section 512 of the Digital Millennium Copyright Act (DMCA). Its purpose is to effect your removal of the infringements listed above.

I have a good faith belief that the use of my copyrighted material as described above has not been authorized by me or any agent acting on my behalf. Please act immediately to remove or to disable access to this infringing material.

I may be contacted at: (your address here)
        Email: aruin@geektravel.com
        Mailing Address: 1501 Barrier Way, Ogden, UT

Sincerely,
Armond Ruin

The DCMA includes copyright infringement complaint procedures. Scan the QR code below to access Twitter's complaint process.

APPENDICES

Privacy and publicity rights are different from copyright interests. Scan the QR code below to access the LOC's distinction between them.

Appendix A: Library of Congress Searches

Copyright, Privacy, and Publicity Rights

Works created by government employees and works performed under government contracts that stipulate they are government works are in the public domain. Since most works on government websites typically fall into one of these two categories, no permission is required to use most screenshots of most government sites. There is one notable exception. Any privately owned and/or licensed material that may be depicted on a government website may require you to seek permission for its use. There should be a notice attached to the content stating that it is not the property of the federal government.

Figure 6 presents the Library of Congress's (LOC) position on copyrights and collections: "It is the researcher's obligation to determine and satisfy copyright or other use restrictions when publishing or otherwise distributing materials found in the Library's collections."

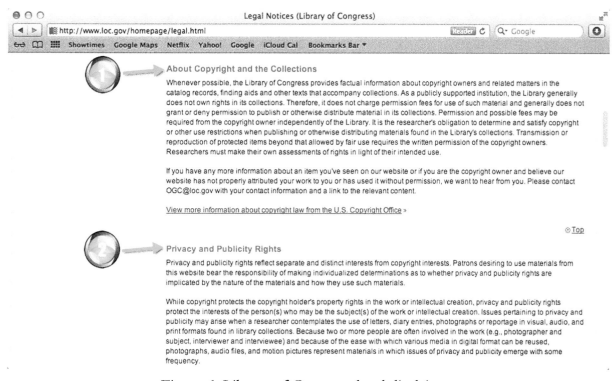

Figure 6: Library of Congress legal disclaimer

(Source: www.loc.gov/homepage/legal.html)

LOC policy regarding copyright and the LOC collections.

LOC policy regarding privacy and publicity rights.

Go to www.loc.gov/rr/print/195_copr.html for information and a thorough discussion, with good examples, of the process for determining rights and restrictions and weighing possible risks on the use of images you find online at the Library of Congress. This is the site for its Prints and Photographs Division.

Library of Congress Website

Figure 7 shows the top portion of the Library of Congress home page, which is an excellent place to start your research. It is the main jumping-off point to access resources and information for authors and publishers.

Figure 7: Library of Congress home page

(Source: www.loc.gov/index.html)

① The URL for the Library of Congress (LOC) website is www.loc.gov.

② The LOC contains collections of historic public domain prints and photographs.

③ A link to the US Copyright Office website is conveniently provided.

④ Clicking the Library Catalogs button will send you to the LOC's Online Catalog, where you may conduct a search using a variety of terms that define a work.

LOC Online Catalog

The LOC Online Catalog provides the option of conducting either a basic or a guided search on a number of variables, as shown in Figure 8. (http://catalog.loc.gov)

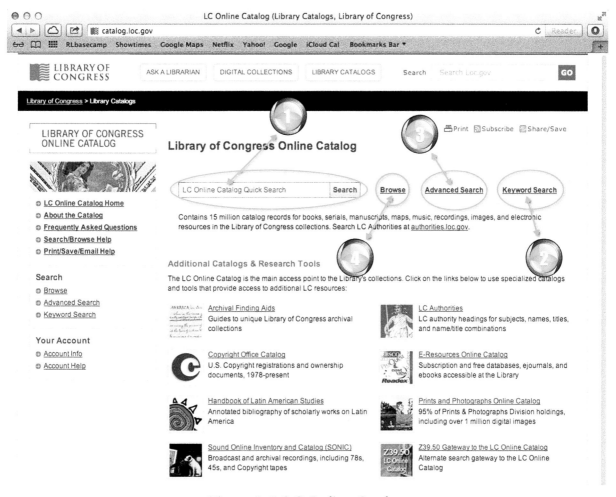

Figure 8: LOC Online Catalog

(Source: http://catalog2.loc.gov)

The quickest way to start is to provide keyword information in the "Quick Search" text block, such as the title of the book and the author's last name.

Choose Keyword Search to yield results on a number of keywords you input into the search block, such as the book title and the author's last name.

Advanced Search allows you to search using up to three sets of complex variables simultaneously.

Selecting the Browse option brings up a new page that allows you to select a single option under the search type, such as the title, the author, or the subject area.

LOC Basic Search

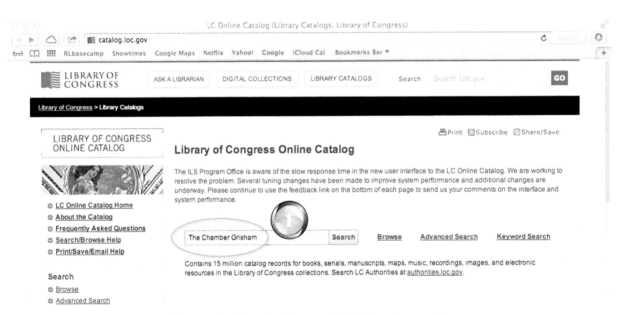

Figure 9: Conducting an LOC basic search

The basic search option was changed during 2012 to make the search process simpler. In the example that follows, the name of a book (*The Chamber*) and only the author's last name (Grisham) are used in the "Quick Search" block. If you use words such as *the* to start the title, you will receive a prompt asking if you want it included or not. In this case, the word *the* was left in the search. Make sure you are listing the exact title since the site will look for exact matches to the terms you use.

LOC Search Results

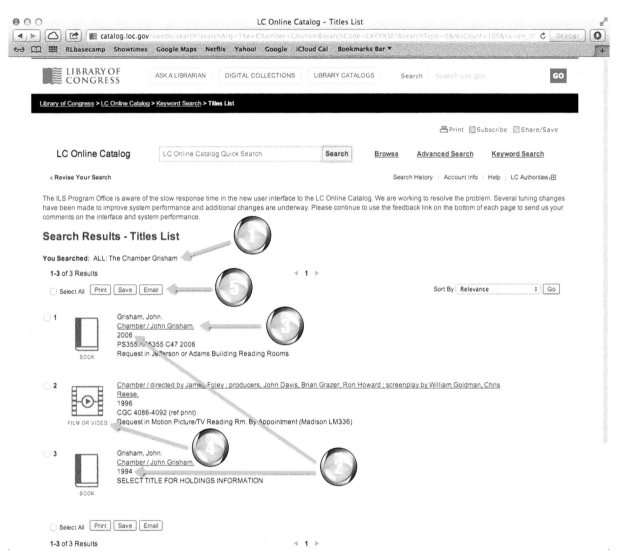

Figure 10: Example of LOC search results

The LOC database includes three entries that exactly matched the three keywords "The," "Chamber," and "Grisham."

Two of the three entries appear to be identical other than the date. One book is from 1994 and the other from 2006.

The full title cells for the 2006 and 1994 entries contain links to the LOC and detailed information in the LOC database related to the keywords that were searched. Figure 11 shows the data for the 1994 date and Figure 12 shows the results when the title with the 2006 date is selected.

The third entry is a motion picture by the same name as the book.

 The site gives options to print, save, or email information, or select all three options.

Database Records

The format of the LOC database records changed during the writing of this workbook. The figures below are screenshots of the most recent version.

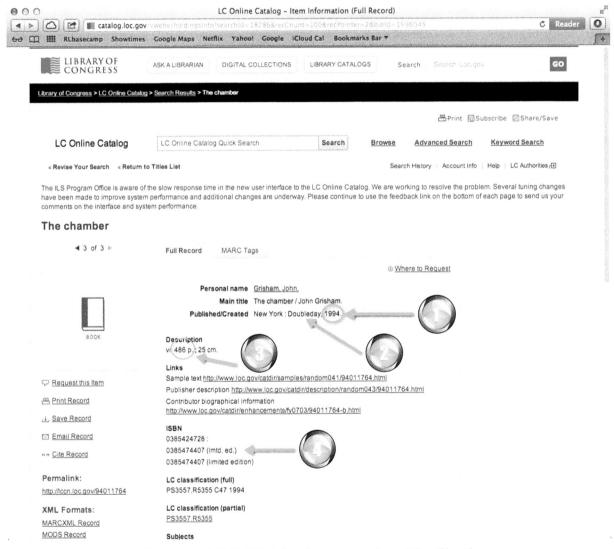

Figure 11: LOC 1994 database record on *The Chamber*

 The LOC database includes data for the 1994 version of *The Chamber* by John Grisham.

The publisher of this edition is Doubleday.

This version of the book has 486 pages. Since the later version has more pages, it is critical to cite the page numbers from the version where you found the content you wish to use when you make a request.

Two different ISBN numbers were assigned to *The Chamber*. One of them was for a limited edition. Both numbers are the old-style ten-digit variety.

How does this information compare to the 2006 entry? See Figure 12.

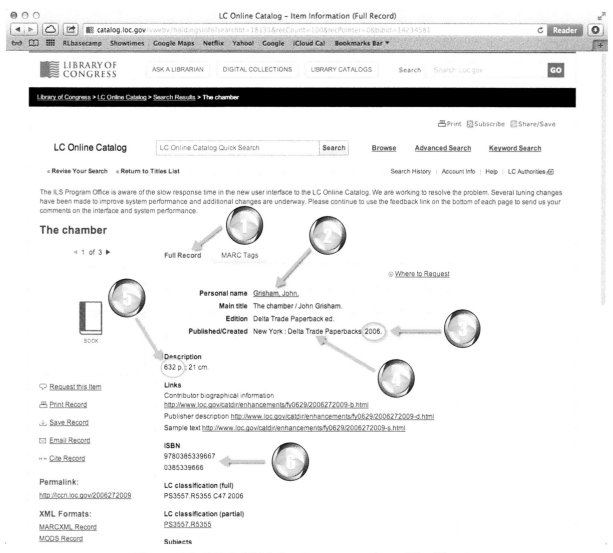

Figure 12: LOC 2006 database record on *The Chamber*

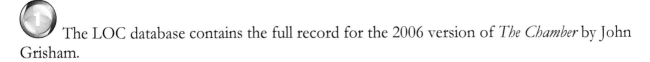 The LOC database contains the full record for the 2006 version of *The Chamber* by John Grisham.

The complete listing of all works by the author may be found by clicking on the name. See Figure 13 for a partial display of John Grisham's listing.

This is the record for the 2006 version of *The Chamber* by John Grisham.

Delta Trade Paperbacks published the book in 2006 in New York.

This 2006 version has 632 pages, compared to 486 pages for the 1994 version. The smaller size of the typical trade edition accounts for the difference.

Two different ISBN numbers were assigned to this version of *The Chamber*. One of them was the old-style ten-digit variety, and the other is the new thirteen-digit variety.

If you use the "Publisher Look-Up Service" on a website of the Association of American Publishers (AAP) to find out more about both publishers, you will learn that both Doubleday and Delta are imprints of Random House. That's where you would go to acquire permission to use quotes from *The Chamber*. (www.publisherlookup.org)

As indicated in Note 2 above, a complete listing of everything attributed to the author is just a couple of clicks away. See Figure 13.

It is interesting to note that the record starts out with four films that are based on Grisham books. Persons other than Grisham wrote all four screenplays.

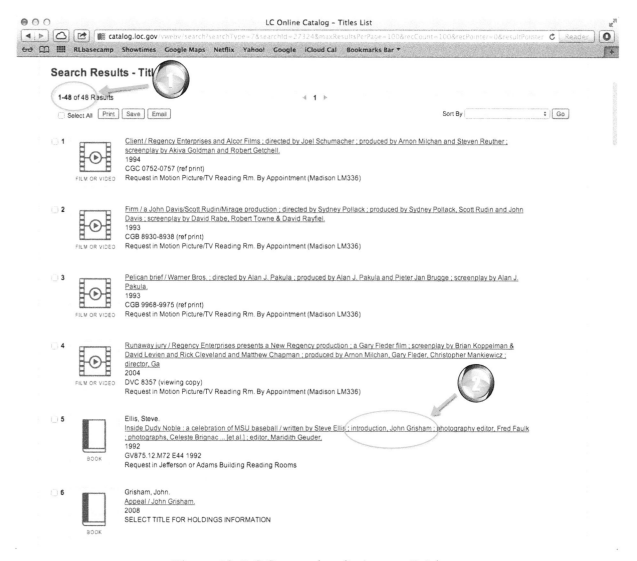

Figure 13: LOC complete listing on Grisham

The LOC includes forty-eight records about works attributed to John Grisham.

The record also includes contributions to works, as illustrated in the introduction that Grisham wrote for the Steve Ellis book *Inside Dudy Noble*.

Copyright Holders

It should be noted that neither record for the example of *The Chamber* indicated who actually holds the copyright on the work. In order to find out who owns the copyright, go to the US Copyright website at www.copyright.gov. A screenshot of the website is presented in Figure 14.

Figure 14: US Copyright Office website

The US Copyright Office has records on who owns the copyright of various works, including books.

The copyright owners may be found by searching "Registrations and Documents" records.

The US Copyright Office website has records of copyrights and documents recorded since January 1978. Clicking on "Registrations and Documents" (see Note 2 above) will send you to the web page (shown in Figure 15) where you may initiate a search of the records. The web page also has suggestions for finding copyright information on works registered prior to January 1, 1978.

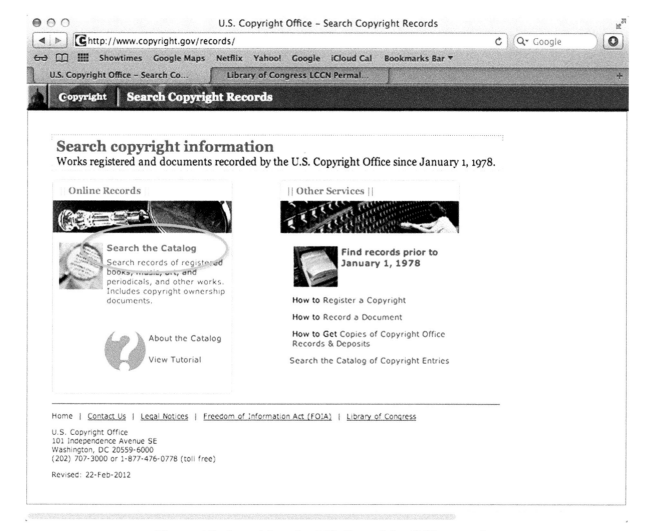

Figure 15: Searching the US Copyright Office catalog

With the changes in the LOC website in 2012, the US Copyright Office basic search web page now looks very different from the LOC basic search web page. There are some important differences in the way the sites function.

See Figure 16 for notes about how to conduct an author search on the US Copyright Office website.

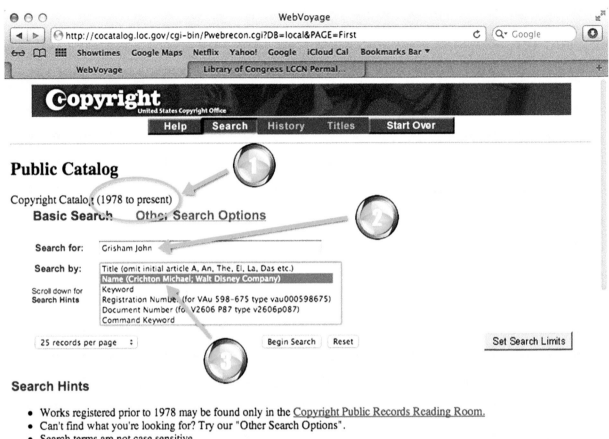

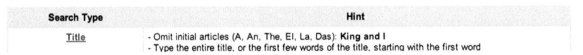

Figure 16: Conduct author searches in the US Copyright Office catalog

The catalog only contains copyrights filed since January 1978.

The author's name must be entered last name then first name, with no punctuation between last and first names.

Highlight the appropriate search parameter in the "Search by" block. In this example, "Name" was used. The example used is "Crichton Michael" for the author and "Walt Disney Company" for a company name. Note that if you list an author's name but leave the default "Title" highlighted, the search will produce no results—unless there happens to be a book titled "Grisham John," which there is not.

The search conducted for John Grisham produced 121 entries, as depicted in Figure 17. The entities are listed alphabetically in the "Full Title" column in the table.

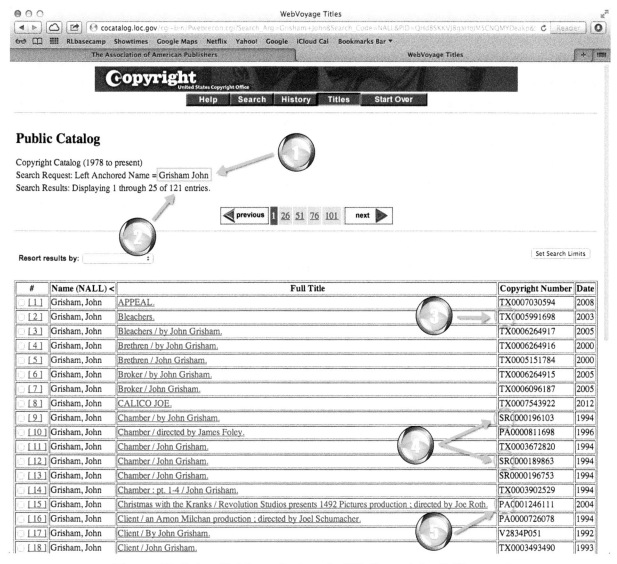

Figure 17: John Grisham listings in US Copyright Office catalog

Verify that the record you obtained is correct.

This indicates the search produced 121 entries.

The TX designation stands for "text," in this case a book in some format. The TX designation can also be used to designate an abridgement of text. In item 14 in the table the abridgement was used for four sound cassettes.

The SR designation is used for Sound Recordings, in this case audiobooks.

The PA designation is used for a Motion Picture attributed to the author and title.

Figure 18 shows that John Grisham owns the copyright to the 1994 edition of the book titled *The Chamber*. The web page screenshot shown in Figure 18 is the result of clicking on item 11 that is shown in Figure 17. If you check some of the other items, such as the motion picture or the sound recordings, you will find that John Grisham does not own the copyright on those items, even though they are based on his book.

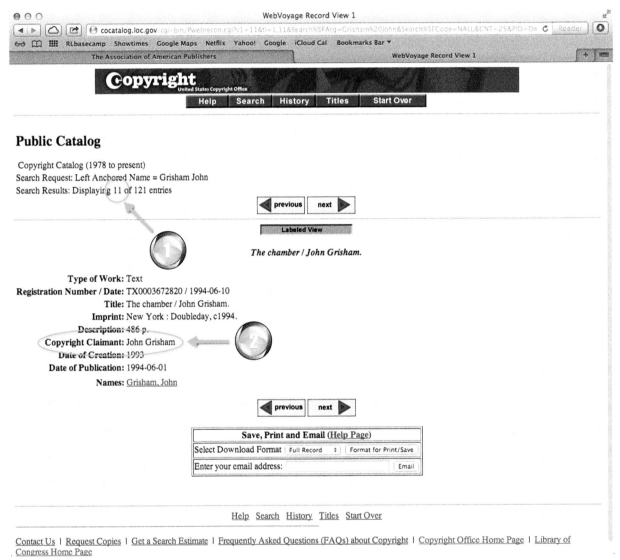

Figure 18: Copyright claimant for *The Chamber*

The information displayed is for item 11 in the previous list (see Figure 17).

John Grisham is the copyright holder for *The Chamber*.

Appendix B: Using Library of Congress Images

In order to determine the copyright status of an image you find on the Library of Congress (LOC) website, find the image you want to use and look at the entry accompanying the image.

The example image presented in Figure 19 may be found at www.loc.gov/pictures/item/fsa1992000242/PP/.

Figure 19: Library of Congress photograph

The accompanying LOC entry for Figure 19 is shown below.

> **Title:** On main street of Cascade, Idaho.
> **Creator(s):** Lee, Russell, 1903-1986, photographer
> **Date Created/Published:** 1941 July
> **Medium:** 1 slide: color.
> **Reproduction Number:** LC-DIG-fsac-1a34209 (digital file from original slide) LC-USF351-212 (color film copy slide)

Rights Advisory: No known restrictions on publication.
Call Number: LC-USF35-212 <P&P> [P&P]
Repository: Library of Congress Prints and Photographs Division Washington, D.C. 20540 USA http://hdl.loc.gov/loc.pnp/pp.print
Notes:

- Transfer from US Office of War Information, 1944.
- General information about the FSA/OWI Color Photographs is available at http://hdl.loc.gov/loc.pnp/pp.fsac
- Title from FSA or OWI agency caption.
- Additional information about this photograph might be available through the Flickr Commons project at www.flickr.com/photos/library_of_congress/2179078530

Subjects:

- Streets
- United States--Idaho--Cascade

Format:

- Slides--Color

Collections:

- Farm Security Administration/Office of War Information Color Photographs

Part of: Farm Security Administration - Office of War Information Collection 11671-15
Bookmark This Record:
www.loc.gov/pictures/item/fsa1992000242/PP/

You can see that beside the entry "Rights Advisory," the US Copyright Office has stated there are "No known restrictions on publication." An explanation of this term from the LOC website is provided below.

"No known restrictions on publication" means that the LOC is unaware of any restrictions on the use of the image. There are generally two cases where this phrase is used:

1. There was a copyright, and it was not renewed.
2. The image is from a late nineteenth or early twentieth century collection for which there is no evidence of any rights holder.

- There are no copyright markings or other indications on any of the images to indicate that they were copyrighted or otherwise restricted, *and*
- The records of the US Copyright Office do not indicate any copyright registration, *and*
- The acquisition paperwork for the collection does not contain any evidence of any restrictions, *and*
- Images from the collection have been used and published extensively without anyone stepping forward to claim rights.

If all the facts are checked under number 2 above, it does not mean the image is in the public domain, but it does indicate that no evidence has been found to show that restrictions apply.

Following the link beside the entry "Collections" will take you to information about the collection from which the image was taken. This information may offer some additional clues as to the rights or rights history of the image. Clicking on the photographer's name and his dates will take you to 20,613 entries!

What follows is a quotation from the LOC website about assessing risks for using historical LOC images:

> *I really want to use an image, but I can't tell for sure that it's ok to use. I don't want to land in jail. What's the worst that might happen to me if I decide to go ahead and publish it?*
>
> The Library is aware of a few cases where a user was told by someone claiming to hold the rights to images in the Library's collections to "cease and desist" publication of the images. When the users requested proof of rights ownership, however, the matter was dropped.
>
> The Library is unaware of any lawsuits involving the use of its historical images.
>
> To establish a prima facie case of copyright infringement, the plaintiff must prove "ownership" of copyright material and "copying" by the defendant. (Norma Ribbon & Trimming, Inc. v. Little, 51 F.3d 45, 47 (5th Cir. 1995) citing Lakedreams v. Taylor, 932 F.2d 1103, 1107 (5th Cir. 1991). A plaintiff establishes "ownership" by demonstrating that the material is "copyrightable" and that he complied with the statutory requirements in securing the copyright. Central Point Software, Inc. v Nugent, 903 F. Supp. 1057 (E.D. Tex. 1995).
>
> If it is difficult for you to find a rights holder after employing due diligence, it ought to be equally difficult for a claimant to show that a copyright had been secured. The U.S. Copyright Law is available online at: www.copyright.gov/title17/circ92.pdf.
>
> (Source: www.loc.gov/rr/print/195_copr.html)

Some images carry the following designation of copyright status: "Publication and other forms of distribution: restricted." Some descriptions state if permission may be acquired, and some have a contact link that points you to a page, providing a way to contact the copyright owner or rights administrator.

Some images carry the statement that they are in the public domain. The description below is an example taken from a rights statement for photographer Carol M. Highsmith from

the Prints and Photographs (P&P) Division on the LOC website at
www.loc.gov/rr/print/res/482_high.html.

Carol M. Highsmith's photographs *are in the public domain.*

Access: Subject to P&P policy on serving originals.

Reproduction (photocopying, hand-held camera copying, photoduplication and other forms of copying allowed by "fair use"): Subject to P&P policy on copying, which prohibits photocopying of the original color photographs.

Publication and other forms of distribution: Ms. Highsmith *has stipulated that her photographs are in the public domain.* (See P&P Collection Files.)

Credit Line: Library of Congress, Prints & Photographs Division, photograph by Carol M. Highsmith [reproduction number, e.g., LC-USZ62-123456]

Appendix C: Determine Online Owner's Positions on Copyright Permission

Below is a good example of a permissions statement about the use of product graphics. It is modeled here to show how to read a "permissions statement," with examples of important items to look for in such a statement. Google has a definite position on copyright regarding its content on the Internet.

Go to www.google.com/permissions/using-product-graphics.html to see the actual page reproduced below. Figure 20 presents an acceptable unaltered screenshot of Google's terms and conditions for reproducing screenshots.

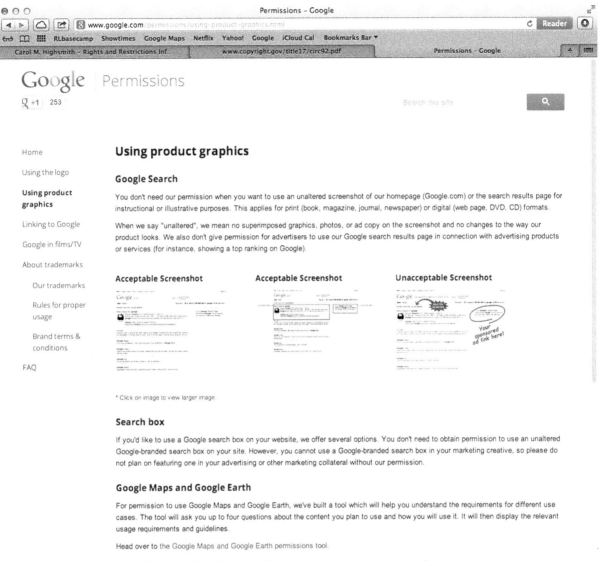

Figure 20: Top of Google's Permissions website

In Figure 21 the highlighted box marked in red with a caption "See notes" follows Google's acceptable use policy. In this example the note provides a statement of exclusion to the general permissions policy regarding Google Maps and Google Earth guidelines.

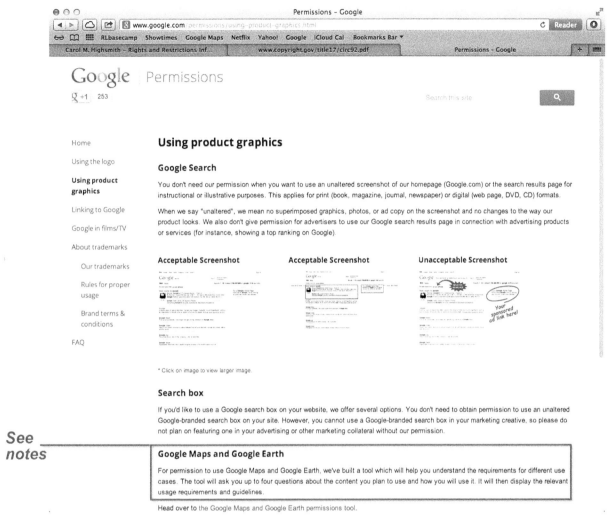

See notes

Figure 21: Illustration of correct modification of a Google screenshot

Since Google now owns YouTube, there is a link on the Google permissions page that goes to the YouTube policy statement about the use of YouTube graphics on other people's websites. This page is shown in Figure 22.

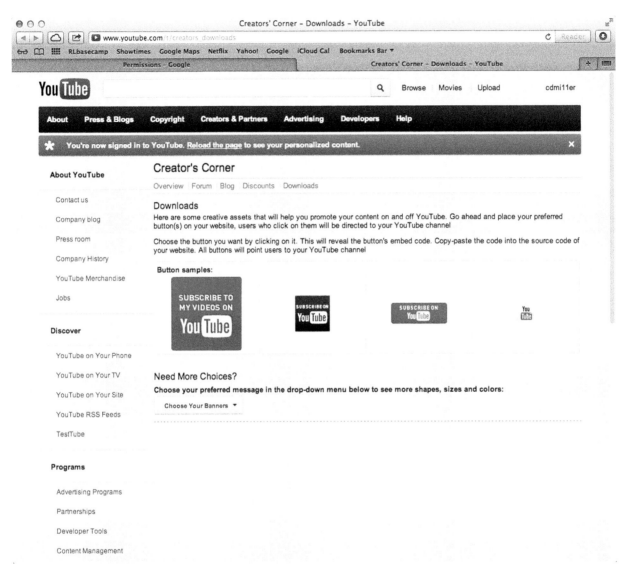

Figure 22: Copyright provisions for YouTube

Appendix D: Sample Request Letters

Sample Request Letter for Use of Text in Print and Electronic Form

The sample letter below is likely sufficient for the purpose of simply reprinting text in a book, newsletter, or other printed matter or for displaying content on your website. For additional information on various media and genre requests, see Chapter 16 on submitting requests with support materials. Many publishers request you fill out an online form, and you may have to begin there instead of writing a letter like the one below. If the administrator is a publisher, check the publisher's website for procedures for submitting such requests and for restrictions on the use of materials before sending a letter.

If you are sending a letter through the US Postal Service, include a self-addressed stamped envelope. Some permissions administrators will ask that the submission materials be faxed instead of mailed.

Permissions
Back Bay Books/Little, Brown and Company
Hatchette Book Group
237 Park Avenue
New York, NY 10017

John Smith
Your Brilliant Publishing Co.
2342 Right Road
Fairbanks, AL 63879

Phone: 303.555.1234   Fax: 303.555.5678
Email: johnsmith@brilliant.com

Permissions:

I am an author of print and electronic materials. I am seeking permission to reproduce the text described below in a book. Please read the following request, fill in the blank spaces, and sign on the space provided or send me via post or email your agreement for my perusal. If you are not the administrator of the rights requested and you know who is, I would appreciate any information regarding the appropriate contacts for my request.

I look forward to hearing from you in the near future. Please contact me with any questions regarding my use.

Request of Permission

> **Nature/title of material:** *Blink: The Power of Thinking without Thinking*
> **Publisher:** Little, Brown and Company
> **Imprint:** Back Bay Books
> **ISBN:** 978-0-316-01066-5 (pb)
> **Number of words in excerpts we wish to reproduce:** 256
> **Copyright dates:** *Little Brown and Company Jan. 2007*
> **Page numbers or other description of material:** from "Afterword," page 259

The above material will be used in the print publication named and in the manner described below:

> **Name of publication:** *Moving Forward © 2013*
> **Number of pages:** 196
> **Price of print publication:** $22
> **Date of publication:** Jan. 24, 2013
> **Nature of publication:** Textbook
> **Edition of publication:** New
> **Format:** Print publication
> **Run of print publication:** 10,000–15,000 copies
> **Language of publication:** English only
> **Photocopy:** A photocopy of the material as it will appear in my book is enclosed.

The above material will be used in the electronic publication named and in the manner described below:

> **Name of publication:** *Moving Forward © 2013*
> **Price:** $35/user
> **Format:** A course management system (possibly Blackboard)
> **Usage date(s):** 2013–2015
> **Overall users:** 5,000

Copyright: Grantor provides publisher with the one-time, English, North American rights to publish cited material in manner cited above. Grantor will retain copyright to rights-held material, save for the permission outlined above. Additional languages, subsequent editions, or use other than indicated above must be permissioned separately by grantee and agreed to by grantor. Permission may not be reused, transferred, assigned, sold, or otherwise disposed by grantee without written consent of grantor.

Fees: If there is a fee associated with the grant of permission, please specify.

One-time fee of: _____

Credit line(s): Credits of granting institutions will be acknowledged within the book. In special circumstances, grantee will entertain or use wording as prescribed by grantor. If you would like me to use a specific credit line, please supply the desired wording below.

Specific credit line: _____

By signature of the granting institution, you agree to the above terms of use and indicate that you are the sole owner of the copyright and/or that you have the right to grant permission to republish the content specified above. Your signature below also indicates that the content discussed above does not infringe upon the rights of any other party.

Sincerely,

John Smith
Author of *Moving Forward*

PERMISSION IS HEREBY GRANTED:

_____

Publisher/Copyright Holder or Legally Appointed Administrator

Name and Title _____

Address _____

Date _____

Sample Request Letter for Images on Website

The sample request below is likely sufficient for the use of an image found on one website for use on another website. This simpler format is easier to use if the only contact information is an email address. If you find a mailing address, you may want to use a more formal format, such as the one in the previous example.

Request Date: June 1, 2011

I am writing to request permission to republish the following item on my website www.WondurMind.com. My phone number is 555-503-1212 and email address is misbrilliant@wondurmind.com.

I intend to use the image I am requesting from March 1, 2013 to July 31, 2013 for a special promotion. The image I wish to use is titled "Biggest Wave Ever" on the home page at www.myhawaiiexperience.com.

Description of Use
The use is a commercial one. I plan to use the image requested above to enhance my description of Hawaii and entice travelers to take my writer's workshop in beautiful Hawaii.

If you do not control the copyright on the above mentioned material, I would appreciate any contact information you can give me regarding the proper rights holder(s), including current address(es). Otherwise, your permission confirms that you hold the right to grant the permission requested here.

Figure 23: Sample request letter for images on website

Appendix E: Sample Grant Letter

You may receive or send a letter like the one below, or you may send or receive a more detailed license to use copyrighted material such as the one outlined in Chapter 8.

January 20, 2009

From: Contracts Manager
The Permission Granting Agency, Inc.
Email: ContractsManager@aol.com

To: Joyce Miller
Your Brilliant Publishing Co.
Email: Joycem@writerservices.biz

Re: Great Author permission (3 items)

Dear Joyce,

We are happy to give Your Brilliant Publishing Company permission to reprint three excerpts from copyrighted material by Great Author. This letter shall serve as an addendum to the attached permission forms you submitted January 20, 2012, by fax. Any license granted for this material is subject to the following terms and conditions:

- Nonexclusive license. North American distribution only. English language only.
- No changes of any kind may be made to the material unless written permission is obtained from the estate of Great Author.
- Term of License limited to materials created for distribution in 2009–2011 only. Print copies shall be limited to 15,000; online end users shall be limited to 5,000.
- Credit must be included as follows: "Reprinted by special arrangement with the estate of Great Author and The Permission Granting Agency, Inc. All rights reserved."
- Subject to a fee of $500 for all three excerpts.

If these terms are acceptable, please have this Agreement signed and returned to me. If you have any questions, please do not hesitate to contact me.

Sincerely,   Agreed and Accepted:

_____   _____
Contracts Manager   Your Brilliant Publishing Co.
The Permission Granting Agency, Inc.   Chief Publishing and Program Officer

YouTube provides guidance on how to manage your rights on their platform. Scan the QR code below to access the website.

Appendix F: Creative Commons License

Creative Commons (CC) is a US nonprofit corporation founded in 2001. It released several copyright licenses in 2002. The original licenses it released granted what they called "baseline rights."

Please check the CC site at www.creativecommons.org for the latest information on these licenses before using works released under a Creative Commons license or before releasing your work under a Creative Commons license. The information below is current as of the publication of this book but may change with time.

There are now six major CC licenses, each with a distinctive graphic. All six require the licensee to credit the original creator of the work. (http://creativecommons.org/licenses/)

In addition, CC now identifies an *unported* or *ported* license. An *unported* license applies internationally, without designation of a specific country where the license will apply. A *ported* license allows the licensor to identify the country (jurisdiction) where the CC license will apply. The CC website provides a website interface that allows the licensor to select among the fifty-six jurisdictions where the CC license will apply.

The details of the rights granted in each CC license depends on the version chosen. Each version of the license is made up of a selection of four conditions.

> **Attribution Licensees:** Allows you to copy, distribute, display, and perform the work and make derivative works based on it only if you give the author or licensor credits in the manner specified in these licenses.
>
> **Noncommercial Licensees:** Allows you to copy, distribute, display, and perform the work and make derivative works based on it only for noncommercial purposes.
>
> **No Derivative Works or NoDerivs Licensees:** Allows you to copy, distribute, display, and perform only verbatim copies of the work, not derivative works based on it.
>
> **ShareAlike Licensee:** Allows you to distribute derivative works only under a license identical to the license that governs the original work.

Some of these conditions can be mixed or matched to form a CC license. For example, a license may allow attribution, be only for noncommercial use, and specify that no derivative can be made of the work. The CC website provides an interface that identifies which of the six licenses is the correct type based on your preferences. The interface will produce the HTML code that may be used on websites to identify the applicable license.

Go to the Flickr website for an example of CC license uses and symbols. People submit photos to this site for sharing and specify the kind of license under which they wish to release their photos. (www.flickr.com/creativecommons/)

CAUTION: If you use someone else's work that is under a Creative Commons license, your whole work containing that licensed work may be subject to the same license and may not be protected from copying. Also, CC licenses are nonrevocable in one sense. Anyone may choose to stop distribution of a work they had placed under CC licenses. However, this will not affect the works that contain material copied from this work while it was under a CC license. This means that you cannot stop someone who has obtained and used your work under a CC license from continuing to use the resulting work even though you have since revoked the CC license. The resulting work may continue to be circulated, whether it is in the form of verbatim copies, copies included in collective works, and/or adaptations of your work.

Appendix G: Tip Sheet

1. Give yourself plenty of time when making requests. Many publishers will tell you it takes six to eight weeks to get a response. Sometimes it takes much longer.
2. Don't forget that you must get separate permissions for each of the formats in which you wish to publish your book. The administrator for print rights may not be the administrator for electronic rights.
3. Don't think because you give credit for someone else's work you don't need to ask for permission.
4. If a work you are using is in the public domain, you will still want to give credit to its creator. Use of another's works without attribution is plagiarism.
5. A work in the public domain in this country may not be in the public domain in another country. If you plan to publish or distribute in another country, it's best to find out what the laws are regarding use of copyrighted works there.
6. Fulfill your obligations regarding any license in a timely manner.
7. Make sure you have considered the licensor's stipulations regarding how the attribution should be written and where it should be placed.
8. Don't forget to keep track of fee payments and copies of agreements. A signed agreement usually must accompany the check for the fee.
9. Don't forget as you do your research to copy the copyright page, acknowledgments page(s), and pages containing the copyrighted content that you might wish to use. This is critical if you do not always have access to the copyrighted source (a library book or a reference book, for example).
10. If you are considering claiming fair use, read the fair use information in Chapter 5 to help determine whether you think your use of a copyrighted item is fair use. Remember, there are no laws that state a certain number of words is a fair use. We are finding that more and more publishers and printers are reluctant to accept work that has incorporated any material on a fair use basis.
11. Try to ascertain whether the party granting you permission really has the right to do so. When the license granted does not stipulate that the person granting permission is the owner or the representative, you may want to ask for a warranty that this party is the owner of the material.
12. Remember that a new work based on an old work that is in the public domain may have copyrights attached to any new parts or treatments such as introductions, new character traits, the addition of new information, etc. A translation of a public domain work may, for example, be copyrighted even though copyright on the original work has expired.
13. If you are posting copyrighted material on your website, be aware that, as stated in tip 5, public domain material in the United States may not be in the public domain in another country. You could be sued in another country for publishing online what is in the U.S. public domain.

14. Use caution when copying anything from the Internet. Always check the accuracy of the quotation and verify the source credited, if you can.
15. Copyright notice on a collective work may not tell you the copyright owner of a specific work in the collection. You may have to contact the owner of the collective work to find out the owner of the specific work in the collection.
16. If you are taking photographs of people you plan to publish, remember to get model releases before or during the photography sessions.
17. If you are interviewing people, remember to get a release to use the content of the interview in the manner you wish to use it. See the examples of releases for interviews in Appendix J.
18. In any photograph you use, remember to check for images of copyrighted articles, trademarks, or people who may sue you for invading their privacy or violating their right of publicity.
19. Read carefully the copyright owner's limitations on content use. This caution relates to the use of content taken from websites as well as from print works and ebooks.
20. Before copying content from websites, carefully read the sites' information regarding their sources and their ability to grant you permission to use their content.
21. For tax purposes, don't forget to keep track of any fees or other expenditures you encounter related to obtaining copyright permissions. You may be able to deduct the cost of this guide and any copyright clearance workshops, for example.

Appendix H: Permissions Tracking Logs

This appendix contains examples of specific permissions tracking logs for the following kinds of content that you may wish to obtain permission to use:

- Text for print
- Text for ebooks
- Graphics and fine art
- Photographs
- Song lyrics
- Periodicals
- Comic strips
- Maps, graphs, and figures

Information you provide about your work will be consistent across each of the types of content requests you might make. The differences in the information you will want to track, as depicted in the various logs, are based on the nature of the content you wish to use.

The Excel spreadsheets that may be used to record your information can be found at www.thecopyrightdetective.com/guide/logs.

Text-Print Tracking Log

TRACKING LOG: Text-Print

Item number

Source title

Author(s)

ISBN or ISSN of source

Copyright holder of item

Copyright holder of source

Publisher

Imprint

Date of publication

Date of copyright

Page number(s) item is on in source

Number of pages in source

Number of words in quote

Method(s) of contact
(online form, email, phone call, letter)

Date of initial contact

Date(s) of follow-up effort(s)

Name(s) of those contacted

Reply date(s)

Results (denied or granted)

Fee for use

Method of payment

Payment date

Rights acquired (territory, language, no. of copies, length of use, etc.)

Conditions

Limitations on Use

Acknowledgments

[If your source is secondary, you will likely need the above information for the original source.]

Text-eBook Tracking Log

TRACKING LOG: Text-eBook

Item number			
Source title			
Author(s)			
ISBN or ISSN of source			
Copyright holder of item			
Copyright holder of source			
Publisher			
Imprint			
Date of publication			
Date of copyright			
Chapter/section item located in source			
Number of pages in source			
Number of words in quote			
Method(s) of contact (online form, email, phone call, letter)			
Date of initial contact			
Date(s) of follow-up effort(s)			
Name(s) of those contacted			
Reply date(s)			
Results (denied or granted)			
Fee for use			
Method of payment			
Payment date			
Rights acquired (territory, language, no. of copies, length of use, etc.)			
Conditions			
Limitations on Use			
Acknowledgments			

[If your source is secondary, you will likely need the above information for the original source.]

Graphics-Fine Art Tracking Log

TRACKING LOG: Graphics & Fine Art

Item number	
Item title, description, credit line	
Artist/Graphic Artist	
Copyright holder of item	
Date of copyright	
Nonpublication source	
Publication source title (Identifier: ISBN, ISSN, URL)	
Date of publication (If website, date of access)	
Page number(s) item is on in source (If website, complete URL)	
Copyright holder of source	
Rights administrator of item	
Method(s) of contact (online form, email, phone call, letter)	
Date of initial contact	
Date(s) of follow-up effort(s)	
Name(s) of those contacted	
Reply date(s)	
Results (denied or granted)	
Supplier of high-res image	
Fee for camera-ready image	
Fee for image use	
Method of payment(s)	
Payment date(s)	
Rights acquired (territory, language, no. of copies, length of use, etc.)	
Conditions	
Limitations on use	
Acknowledgments	

[If your source is secondary, you will likely need the above information for the original source.]

Photography Tracking Log

TRACKING LOG: Photographs

Item number

Item title, description, credit line

Photographer

Copyright holder of item

Date of copyright

Nonpublication source

Publication source title
(Identifier: ISBN, ISSN, URL)

Date of original publication of item
Date of publication of source

Page number(s) item is on in source
(If website, complete URL)

Copyright holder of source

Rights administrator of item

Method(s) of contact
(online form, email, phone call, letter)

Date of initial contact

Date(s) of follow-up effort(s)

Name(s) of those contacted

Reply date(s)

Results (denied or granted)

Supplier of high-res image

Fee for royalty-free package

Fee for image use

Method of payment(s)

Payment date(s)

Rights acquired (territory, language, no. of copies, length of use, etc.)

Conditions/Contents of photo

Model release(s), trademark(s)

Limitations on use

Acknowledgments

[If your source is secondary, you will likely need the above information for the original source.]

Song Lyrics Tracking Log

TRACKING LOG: Song Lyrics

Item number			
Song title			
Songwriter(s) (list all writers)			
Number of lines			
Copyright holder(s) of item			
Publisher/Administrator(s)			
Date of publication			
Date of copyright			
Method(s) of contact (online form, email, phone call, letter)			
Date of initial contact			
Date(s) of follow-up effort(s)			
Name(s) of those contacted			
Reply date(s)			
Results (denied or granted)			
Fee for use			
Method of payment			
Payment date			
Rights acquired (territory, language, no. of copies, length of use, etc.)			
Conditions			
Limitations on use			
Acknowledgments			

[If your source is secondary, you will likely need the above information for the original source.]

Periodicals Tracking Log

TRACKING LOG: Periodicals

Item number			
Title of article			
Author(s)			
Source of article if not publisher (e.g., AP)			
Copyright date of source if not publisher			
Copyright holder(s), administrator of rights			
Page number(s) of article in source			
Number of words in quote(s)			
Title of periodical			
Publication date of periodical			
Volume and number of periodical			
If online publication, complete URL			
Publisher/copyright holder of periodical			
Association name if publisher			
Membership in association?			
Discounted fee for members			
Method(s) of contact (online form, email, phone call, letter)			
Date of initial contact			
Date(s) of follow-up effort(s)			
Name(s) of those contacted			
Reply date(s)			
Results (denied or granted)			
Fee for use			
Method of payment			
Payment date			
Rights acquired (territory, language, no. of copies, length of use, etc.)			
Conditions			
Limitations on use			
Acknowledgments			

[If your source is secondary, you will likely need the above information for the original source.]

Comic Strip Tracking Log

TRACKING LOG: Comic Strip

Item number

Source title of strip or illustration

Creator of strip or illustration

Copyright holder of item

Date of copyright

Page number(s) item is on in source
(If website, complete URL)

Syndicate

Publication
(If website, URL)

Date of publication
(If website, date of access)

Copyright holder of source

Rights administrator of item

Supplier of high-res image(s)

Fee for camera-ready image

Method(s) of contact
(online form, email, phone call, letter)

Date of initial contact

Date(s) of follow-up effort(s)

Name(s) of those contacted

Reply date(s)

Results (denied or granted)

Fee for use

Method of payment

Payment date

Rights acquired (territory, language, no. of copies, length of use, etc.)

Conditions

Limitations on use

Acknowledgments

[If your source is secondary, you will likely need the above information for the original source.]

Maps, Graphs & Figures Tracking Log

TRACKING LOG: Maps, Graphs & Figures

Item number

Item title, description, credit line

Creator

Copyright holder of item

Date of copyright

Nonpublication source

Publication source title
(Identifier: ISBN, ISSN, URL)

Date of publication
(If website, date of access)

Page number(s) item is on in source
(Ref. #, ID #, complete URL)

Copyright holder of source

Rights administrator of item

Method(s) of contact
(online form, email, phone call, letter)

Date of initial contact

Date(s) of follow-up effort(s)

Name(s) of those contacted

Reply date(s)

Results (denied or granted)

Supplier of high-res image(s)

Fee for camera-ready image

Fee for image use

Method of payment(s)

Payment date(s)

Rights acquired (territory, language,
no. of copies, length of use, etc.)

Conditions

Limitations on use

Acknowledgments

[If your source is secondary, you will likely need the above information for the original source.]

Creative Commons provides a way to grant permission for others to use your works. Scan the QR code below to access the website.

Appendix I: Model Releases

Digital versions of the model release samples below may be found at
www.thecopyrightdetective.com/guide/releases.

Example Model Release

For consideration that I acknowledge, I grant to _____
(Company) and Company's assigns, licensees, and successors, the right to use my
image for all purposes, including advertising, trade, or any other commercial purpose
throughout the world and in perpetuity. I waive the right to inspect or approve
versions of my image used for publication or the written copy that may be used in
connection with the images.

I release the Company and Company's assigns, licensees, and successors from any
claims that may arise regarding the use of my image, including any claims of
defamation, invasion of privacy, or infringement of moral rights, rights of publicity, or
copyright. Company is permitted, although not obligated, to include my name in a
credit in connection with this image.

Company is not obligated to utilize any of the rights granted in this Agreement.

I have read and understood this Agreement, and I am over the age of 18. This
Agreement expresses the complete understanding of the parties.

Print Name: _____

Signature: _____

Address: _____

_____

Date: _____

Example Model Release for Minors
if model is under the age of 18

For consideration that I acknowledge, I grant to _____ (Company) and Company's assigns, licensees, and successors, the right to use my image for all purposes, including advertising, trade, or any other commercial purpose throughout the world and in perpetuity. I waive the right to inspect or approve versions of my image used for publication or the written copy that may be used in connection with the images.

I release the Company and Company's assigns, licensees, and successors from any claims that may arise regarding the use of my image, including any claims of defamation, invasion of privacy or infringement of moral rights, rights of publicity, or copyright. Company is permitted, although not obligated, to include my name in a credit in connection with this image.

Company is not obligated to utilize any of the rights granted in this Agreement.

This Agreement expresses the complete understanding of the parties.

Model Consent

Print Minor's Name: _____

Minor's Signature: _____

Date: _____

Parent/Guardian Consent

Print Parent/Guardian Name: _____

Parent/Guardian Signature: _____

Parent/Guardian Address:

_____

_____

Date: _____

Appendix J: Interview Releases

Many authors prefer to use a simple version of an interview release form such as the first example below, which more interviewees may be willing to sign.

> ## Example Interview Release Form 1
>
> I, _____, was interviewed by _____. I hereby grant him/her permission to use any quotations taken from this interview in his/her book titled _____ (the Work) or in any republication, reprint, or promotion of the Work, including publicity releases in all media formats. I grant him permission to use these quotations in the Work when it is published in any format including print, electronic, or audiobook, or in any format that makes use of any and all future technologies.
>
> Print Name: _____
>
> Signature: _____
>
> Date: _____

If you wish to include an item regarding compensation, you may want to use the model below. Though copies of the work may suffice as consideration, monetary compensation for permission may offer greater protection to the interviewer in any legal action brought against him/her.

Example Interview Release Form 2

I, _____, was interviewed by _____ on _____. I hereby grant him/her permission to use any quotations taken from this interview in his/her book titled _____ (the Work) or in any republication, reprint, or promotion of the book, including publicity releases. I grant him/her permission to use these quotations in the Work when it is published in any format, including print, electronic, or audiobook, or in any format that makes use of any and all future technologies in consideration of _____, receipt of which I hereby acknowledge. (Note: You may wish to offer as compensation either a specific number of copies of the work or monetary compensation or both.)

Print Name: _____

Signature: _____

Date: _____

Caution: If the topic of the interview is in any way controversial, you may wish to include a statement warranting that the interviewee has not divulged any information given to him/her in confidence and/or that all of the interviewee's comments are true. You may want to add the statement in the block below to either of the sample forms above. (You may wish to consult an attorney for help in creating a form when writing and interviewing regarding controversial topics.)

I hereby confirm that during this interview, I made no statements that disclosed information given to me in confidence and that all statements I made during this interview are true.

Glossary: Explanation of Terms Used

Actual Damages
Compensation for losses that can be readily proven to have occurred (see Statutory Damages).

Attribution
Identification of the original source. Providing attribution is an act that may strengthen a fair use claim in a copyright infringement case.

Copyright Infringement
When someone without permission or license to do so exercises any of the five exclusive rights attached by US copyright law to a copyrighted work belonging to another.

Click Wrap License
An onscreen agreement covering the use of a copyrighted work that requires the clicking of a button by the user as an indication of acceptance of its terms.

DMCA (Digital Millennium Copyright Act)
This act is part of US copyright law. It addresses the rights and obligations of owners of copyrighted material and the procedures for having infringements removed from infringer's publications. It also addresses the rights and obligations of Internet service providers.

DRM
Digital Rights Management
A term for technologies that control access in order to limit the uses of digital content and devices to only those which the content owner and/or provider deem acceptable.

Gratis
If you have been granted permission gratis, you are not being charged a fee for the rights to use the copyrighted item in the manner described in the gratis agreement.

Most Favored Nations Clause
A promise by a licensee that he/she will treat one licensor in a manner equal to his/her treatment of another licensor of substantially similar content on the same project. Example: The fee paid for use of some number of lines from a play requiring most favored nations treatment must be at least equal to the fee paid for the same number of lines from any other play used in the same project.

Nonexclusive Rights
When you have been granted nonexclusive rights to use a copyrighted item, others may be granted the permission to use the item in the same way and at the same time you are using it.

Paraphrase
Paraphrasing is making alterations in another author's words. Some copyright licenses disallow any kind of paraphrasing. Paraphrasing may be found to be copyright infringement if there is a "substantial" amount of it. There is no amount or percentage of change set by copyright law to use as a guide for determining substantiality—that is, to determine if enough content is being altered by someone to make them guilty of infringing.

Plagiarism
The pretense by someone that they are the originator of a work they did not create; sometimes called *literary theft*. The work "stolen" by a plagiarist may or may not be copyrighted.

Rights Managed
A rights managed photograph or image is one that may be obtained for a very specific purpose for a specific fee. If the image or photograph is to be used for any other purpose, additional fees typically are applied when the additional license is acquired. The license may be either for exclusive or nonexclusive rights to the image or photograph for the intended purpose.

Royalty Free
This term does not mean copyright free. It does not normally mean that no cost is attached to the use of items under the license. Normally, a royalty-free collection of clip art, photographs, etc., is offered to the purchaser to use in the manner set out in its license. The use has definite limitations, and once the purchaser pays an upfront fee, he/she may use the items in the collection only in the manner described by the license. The purchaser ordinarily does not have to go back to the creator or owner and pay for each time the content in the collection is used.

Statutory Damages
These are damages that are determined by a court of law for copyright infringement. Courts have considerable latitude in assessing awards, which can be between $750 and $150,000 per incidence of infringement. Court costs and legal fees may also be considered in awarding statutory damages.

Stock Photo Services
These services offer licensed photos for specific purposes. Such services have in their collections many photographs and offer licenses for specified fees to cover categories of uses. Two types of licenses that such services offer are rights managed and royalty free. See the definitions of these two types above.

US Copyright
A bundle of five exclusive rights allowed by US copyright law to a creator of a work. These exclusive rights are listed below.

1. The right to reproduce the work
2. The right to distribute copies of the work to the public
3. The right to perform the work publicly
4. The right to display the work publicly
5. The right to create derivative works based on the original work

Purchasers of this book may download Excel versions of the permissions tracking logs identified above. The password may be obtained by registering the purchase. Scan the QR code below to access the registration webpage.

Copyright Cases

Fairey v. Associated Press

Fairey v. Associated Press, No. 09-CV-01123, (S.D.N.Y. complaint filed 2/9/ 2009)

Visual artist Shepard Fairey created an image based on an Associated Press (AP) photo of Barack Obama. This image, titled the *Hope Image*, became popular during the presidential campaign of 2008. It was placed on posters, buttons, and fliers.

Eventually, AP complained that Fairey had used the photo without permission. Fairey sued AP for a declaratory judgment that his use was a fair use. The two sides eventually settled. Both will share the *Hope Image* going forward, and Fairey has agreed to never again use an AP photo in his artwork without a license. The terms of the financial settlement were not disclosed.

Rogers v. Koons

Rogers v. Koons, 960 F.2d 301 (2d Cir. 1992)

Jeff Koons created a sculpture based on a popular photo by Art Rogers of a couple holding several puppies. Koons claimed the work was a parody of the original work—a commentary on the banality of everyday items. The court decided Koons was guilty of copyright infringement. This attempt at claiming a fair use failed.

Bridgeman Art Library v. Corel Corporation

Bridgeman Art Library, Ltd. v. Corel Corporation, 36 F. Supp. 2d 191 (S.D.N.Y. 1999)

Bridgeman had obtained rights from hundreds of museums to photograph public domain masterpieces from various museums. Corel allegedly published 150 of them without asking Bridgeman's permission.

The court decided that if a photograph produces an exact image of a public domain painting, it by nature lacks originality and is a slavish copy and therefore not copyrightable.

However, this decision was made by a federal district court trial judge, and other courts are not held to this decision.

So, the answer to the sticky question "Is it okay to copy a photo of a public domain image?" is that no one can say for sure presently whether a work containing such a photo will or will not be held in a court of law to be an infringement.

J. D. Salinger v. Colting

Salinger v. Colting, 641 F. Supp. 2d 250 (S.D.N.Y. 2009), vacated 607 F. 3d 68 (2d Cir. 2010).

Frederik Colting wrote an unofficial "sequel" to J. D. Salinger's *Catcher in the Rye,* titled *60 Years Later: Coming Through the Rye,* and claimed the work was a parody. A U.S. judge granted a preliminary injunction and concluded the new book was an infringement because it continued *The Catcher in the Rye* story without turning it into something new (therefore not transformative). The injunction blocked the publication and distribution of the new book. The court found the taking of the primary character, the attributes of the character, and a similar and often repetitive story line amounted to taking too much.

The court found also that the new work could have a negative effect on the market for Salinger's work.

> [W]hile it appears unlikely that '60 Years' would undermine the market for 'Catcher' itself, it is quite likely that the publishing of '60 Years' and similar widespread works could substantially harm the market for a 'Catcher' sequel or other derivative works, whether through confusion as to which is the true sequel or companion to 'Catcher,' or simply because of reduced novelty or press coverage.

Salinger v. Colting, 641 F. Supp. 2d 250, 268 (S.D.N.Y. 2009).

Settlement
Colting appealed and the Second Circuit Court of Appeals vacated the preliminary injunction and remanded the case to the district court. The Second Circuit remanded because it held the test used by the district court for fair use and infringement in this case was not a proper test in light of the 2006 Supreme Court Decision in eBay v. MercExchange, 547 U.S. 388.
Salinger v. Colting, 607 F. 3d 68 (2d Cir. 2010).

The Second Circuit did agree however that Salinger was likely to win the suit if the case went to trial. The estate of J. D. Salinger and Frederik Colting reached an agreement regarding the publishing of the Colting work. It allows Colting to publish the book in some international territories but not in the United States until the original work falls into the public domain.

Cooks Source Controversy

In 2010 Monica Gaudio wrote an article on the medieval origins of apple pie and published it on her website. Later, a friend wrote to congratulate her on having it published in a regional magazine titled *Cooks Source*. It was published in both the online and print versions of the magazine. Gaudio complained that her article was published without her permission. In an answer to her complaint about the infringement, she said, the magazine sent her an email telling her that what is on the Internet is public domain and that she should be happy with the magazine for cleaning up her mistakes. There was a hue and cry on the Internet as bloggers and news sources shared the information about the *Cooks Source* controversy. The magazine eventually took down its Facebook page and suffered much bad publicity from this incident.

Extradition of United Kingdom student, Richard O'Dwyer

The United States Department of Justice has sought the extradition to the U.S. of Richard O'Dwyer, a United Kingdom student, to face charges of copyright violations. His website provided links to sites that infringed copyright by streaming without license copyrighted TV shows produced mostly in the US. A British judge had ruled that the extradition could go ahead. O'Dwyer appealed to Britain's High Court and the appeal was heard at the Royal Courts of London in the summer of 2012.

On November 28, 2012, the High Court announced that Mr. O'Dwyer will not be extradited to the United States to face trial and possible imprisonment. Instead, he signed an agreement and will pay a small sum in compensation for his infringement.

Purchasers of this book may download MS Word versions of the sample model releases identified above. Scan the QR code below to access the webpage.

Resources

Bible Gateway, The: (www.biblegateway.com)
>   This is a source for a list of versions and translations of the Bible. Links on this site lead to rights information that can be very helpful in permissions acquisition.

Copyright Basics (Circular 1) by US Copyright Office (www.copyright.gov/circs/circ01.pdf)

Copyright Clearance Center, The (www.copyright.com)
>   CCC offers collective clearance services for primarily academic and corporate users (textbook publishers and authors).

Copyright consulting services (http://TheCopyrightDetective.com)

Copyright Handbook: What Every Writer Needs to Know, The by Stephen Fishman, JD (www.nolo.com/products/the-copyright-handbook-COHA.html)
>   This book offers an extensive coverage of copyright law covering many aspects of copyright from transfers of ownership of copyright to profiting from intellectual property.

Getting Permission: How to Clear Copyrighted Materials Online & Off by Attorney Richard Stim
>   A comprehensive guide to clearing rights including extensive coverage of license and merchandise agreements, academic permissions and music licensing.

Graphic Artists Guild Handbook: Pricing & Ethical Guidelines (www.graphicartistsguild.org/handbook/)

Library of Congress website at http://loc.gov and http://loc.gov/index.html
>   The Library of Congress's principal mission is to research inquiries made by members of Congress. It is open to the public, but only members of Congress, employees, Supreme Court Justices and other high-ranking government officials can check out books. Its website offers creators a wealth of information and access to an ever expanding treasure trove of content such as photographs, artwork, film and print works as more and more materials are digitized and added to the collections placed online.

Little Book of Plagiarism, The by Richard A. Posner
>   A brief overview and exploration of plagiarism, defining the term, giving current examples, and discussing how the current view of it developed and how perceptions of it have changed during its history. Its author is a well-known and highly respected legal scholar.

Plagiarism Today (www.plagiarismtoday.com)

> A website focused on the issues of plagiarism online. Its host, Jonathan Bailey, explains on the site that he is not an attorney and that this is not to be considered a legal blog. The purpose is to inform webmasters and copyright holders.

Public Domain: How to Find & Use Copyright-Free Writings, Music, Art & More, The by Stephen Fishman, JD (www.nolo.com/products/the-public-domain-PUBL.html)

> This work is a comprehensive guide to locating and accessing copyright free writings, music, art, photography, software, maps, databases, and videos.

Public Domain Publishing Bible: How to Create "Royalty" Income for Life, The by Andras M. Nagy (www.thepublicdomainbible.com/)

> A guide offering advice on how to republish public domain books.

US Copyright Office (www.copyright.gov)

> The Copyright Office is an office of record for copyright registration and deposit of copyright material. The Copyright Office website contains information on and the means to registers copyright and deposit materials. It offers a means of searching copyright registrations for the years 1978 and beyond.

Example of Images and Their Sources

Public Domain Images Created by Government Employees

Historical Photographs

A tremendous wealth of photographs and information is available from the Library of Congress website at www.loc.gov/pictures/. Figure 24 shows one of the most frequently used images out of the 175,000 black-and-white photographs available through the Library of Congress. This one is in the Farm Security Administration's Photography Collection titled *Migrant Mother*, taken by Dorothea Lange in 1936. The federal Resettlement Administration, later called the Farm Security Administration, employed Lange during the Great Depression.

Figure 24: Migrant Mother

Title: *Migrant Mother*
Photo Credit: Dorothea Lange
Date Created: 1936
Collection: Farm Security Administration/Office of War Information
Source: www.loc.gov/pictures/item/fsa1998021539/PP/

Figure 25: Historical photograph created by a government employee

Title: Members of the US Geological and Geographical Survey of the Territories (Hayden Survey), 1870
Photo Credit: William Henry Jackson
Date Created: 1870
Collection: US Geological Survey Photographic Library
Source: http://libraryphoto.cr.usgs.gov/htmlorg/lpb002/land/jwh00282.jpg

Wyoming. Photo of all the members of the US Geological and Geographical Survey of the Territories, made while in camp at Red Buttes at the junction of the North Platte and Sweetwater Rivers. Standing left to right: John "Potato John" Raymond and "Val," cooks; Sanford R. Gifford, landscape painter; Henry W. Elliott, artist; James Stevenson, assistant; H. D. Schmidt, naturalist; E. Campbell Carrington, zoologist; L. A. Bartlett, general assistant; and William Henry Jackson, photographer for the Survey. Sitting left to right: C. S. Turnbull, secretary; J. H. Beaman, meteorologist; Ferdinand.V. Hayden, geologist in charge; Cyrus Thomas, agriculturist; Raphael, hunter; and A. L. Ford, mineralogist.

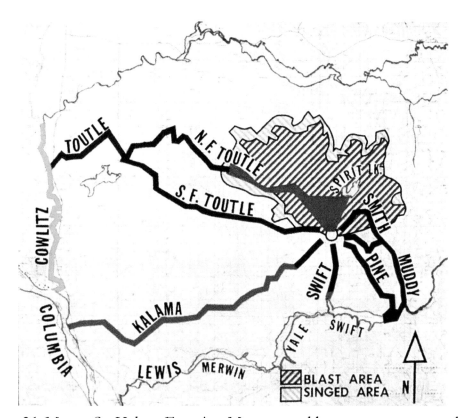

Figure 26: Mount St. Helens Eruption Map, created by a government employee

Title: ID. CVO-A. 6ct
Date Created: 1980
Collection: US Geological Survey Photography Library
Source: http://libraryphoto.cr.usgs.gov/cgi-bin/show_picture.cgi?ID=ID. CVO-A. 6ct

Current Photographs

Figure 27: Photograph created by a government employee

Title: *Indiana Bat*
Photo Credit: Susi von Oettingen, Endangered Species Biologist for the US Fish and Wildlife Service
Date Created: June 13, 2011
Collection: US Fish and Wildlife Service, National Digital Library
Source:
http://digitalmedia.fws.gov/cdm4/item_viewer.php?CISOROOT=/natdiglib&CISOPTR=128
81&CISOBOX=1&REC=3

Public Domain Copyright-Expired Images

Figure 28: Example of a copyright-expired image

Artist: Sir John Tenniel
Image scanned from 1800s copy of Lewis Carroll's *Alice in Wonderland*

Figure 29: Example of a copyright-expired image

Title: Dorothy meets the Cowardly Lion
From: *The Wonderful Wizard of Oz*, first edition
Illustrator: W. W. Denslow
Date Created: Circa 1900
Source: Library of Congress LC Control No.: 03032405 (p.81)
http://en.wikipedia.org/wiki/File:Cowardly_lion2.jpg

Public Domain Photographs

Figure 30: Example of a photograph placed in the public domain

Title: *Iguanas on the Tree*
Photo Credit: Anna Langova
Date Created: July 19, 2008
Source: www.publicdomainpictures.net/view-image.php?image=922

Figure 31: Example of an image from a library collection

Title: Compliments of W. F. Cody to Mrs. Nate Salsbury Paris 1889
Collection: Salsbury Collection, Buffalo Bill's Wild West Show
Call Number: NS-15, Western History/Genealogy Dept., Denver Public Library
Source:
http://digital.denverlibrary.org/cdm/singleitem/collection/p15330coll22/id/78811/rec/1

Public Domain Images from Historical Societies

Figure 32: Example of an image from a historical society

Title: *Band Saw in Keene New Hampshire*
Creator: Bion Whitehouse
Publisher: Keene Public Library and the Historical Society of Cheshire County
Date Created: 1900–1920?
Rights Management: No known copyright restrictions.
Source: www.flickr.com/photos/keenepubliclibrary/7308330284/in/photostream

Images Used Under Creative Commons License

Figure 33: Example of a Creative Commons image

Title: Mormon Row Barns
Date: June 19, 2004
Source: www.pdphoto.org/PictureDetail.php?mat=&pg=8163

Clip Art Images

Figure 34: Example of a free clip art image

Source: http://missmary.com/wp-content/uploads/2012/02/easter-cherubs-egg-yp1888.jpg

Stock Photo Images

Figure 35: Example of a purchased stock image

Rights Management: Royalty-free stock photograph, nonexclusive sublicense
Source: http://us.fotolia.com/id/7082007

Copyrighted Website Screen Captures

Figure 36: Example of a website screen capture

Images from Private Collections

Figure 37: Example of an image from a private collection

Collection: Cynthia Holder Collection
Date Created: Circa 1940
Rights Management: Copyrighted content. Courtesy of Cynthia Holder.

Fine Art Images

Figure 38: Example of a fine art image

Title: *Harvest*
Artist: Michael Miller
Medium: Acrylic on canvas
Date Created: Circa 1995
Photo Credit: Michael Miller
Date Created: Circa 1998
Rights Management: Copyrighted content. Used with permission.

Cartoons

Figure 39: Example of a cartoon

Title: 19460
Creator: Stan Yan
Date Created: Sept. 7, 2006
Rights Management: Copyrighted 2006 Stan Yan. Used with permission.
Source: www.webcomicsnation.com/StanYan/tickletape/series.php?view=single&ID=19460

The QR codes presented in this book were generated by QRStuff.com. Scan the QR code below to access the website.

Index

Authors

Joyce L. Miller

Joyce is a co-founder and co-owner of Integrated Writer Services, LLC, a publishing consulting service. Joyce is a consultant to independent publishers and their support teams, an author, and an educator with over twenty years experience in publishing, copyright, and copyright compliance. She has served as intellectual property manager, first for NASA's Classroom of the Future, and later for the Center for Educational Technologies, NASA's principal research and development center for educational technologies. She has served as associate editor for an academic/trade technology journal, *The Technology Transfer Journal.*
Joyce has created and been instrumental in the oversight of policies encompassing best practices, processes and procedures for copyright compliance issues at the university level as well as at government research and development centers.

Dr. C. Daniel Miller

Dan is a co-founder and co-owner of Integrated Writer Services, LLC, an independent publishing consulting service. He has served as vice president and president of the Colorado Independent Publishers Association (CIPA). He currently consults on the business of independent publishing. He has been a technology consultant to architects to design computer and telecommunications infrastructures. He was the founding president of the Center for Educational Technologies; the executive director of NASA's Classroom of the Future; a university professor and university department chair; an
educational researcher, a K-12 classroom teacher, and a US Air Force radar technician. He most recently has embarked on a new venture as a project manager and researcher to discover relevance in large unstructured data.

Visit www.facebook.com/TheCopyrightDetective for the latest information about the authors and what is happening in the world of copyright.

Customized Workshops Available

The authors of this guide offer customized workshops and presentations on copyright and permission acquisition to writers groups, independent publishing organizations, and trade associations related to the publishing industry.

Time allocation: one to three hours
Location: to be determined by the group
Fees: negotiable, plus travel and expenses
Guide: Participants will receive a print copy of the *Copyright Clearance for Creatives* along with a CD-ROM with updated version with active hyperlinks.

Contact Joyce Miller at joyce@thecopyrightdetective.com to discuss how we can customize a presentation or workshop for your organization, association, or group.

Copyright Clearance Consulting Services

Integrated Writer Services, LLC (IWS) provides consulting services for writers of both fiction and nonfiction works who intend to publish their works independently or through small presses, independent publishers, traditional publishers, or print-on-demand (POD) publishers.

IWS will consider discounts for larger copyright clearance projects (i.e., hundreds of individual items). A minimum of one hour consulting is required. For rates and information about setting up a consultation, contact Joyce Miller at joyce@thecopyrightdetective.com.

Digital Resources Available

Purchasers of the print version of this guide may obtain complimentary digital versions of templates, forms, and examples by registering at www.TheCopyrightDetective.com/guide/registration/.